Behind the Looking-Glass

Reflections on the Myth of Lewis Carroll

by Sherry L. Ackerman

evertype

2012

Published by Evertype, Cnoc Sceichín, Leac an Anfa, Cathair na Mart, Co. Mhaigh Eo, Éire. *www.evertype.com*.

First published by Cambridge Scholars Publishing (Newcastle), 2008.
  ISBN 978-1-84718-486-3

A catalogue record for this book is available from the British Library.

ISBN-10 1-78201-017-3
ISBN-13 978-1-78201-017-3

Typeset in De Vinne Text, Mona Lisa, ENGRAVERS' ROMAN, and *Liberty* by Michael Everson.

Cover: Michael Everson.

Printed by LightningSource.

Foreword

He does not then choose to conceal the truth; what he used to do was to give a twist to its manifestation, which, like a beam of light, is refracted more than once in its passage, and is parted into many rays as it becomes poetry, and so to remove whatever in it was harsh and hard. Tyrants might thus be left in ignorance, and enemies not forewarned. For them he threw a veil in the innuendoes and ambiguities which hid the meaning from others, but he did not elude the intelligence of the actual consultants who gave their whole mind to the answers... —Plutarch XXVI

The fact Lewis Carroll's newest biographer betrayed a complete unawareness of his involvement in Esoteric Buddhism, even though that involvement was the central them of his last novel *Sylvie & Bruno*, is only the most recent, not the most egregious example of how badly served his complex religious and spiritual life has been by his many Boswells. Like almost every other aspect of his existence, the image of Lewis Carroll as a religious conservative is largely a myth, and it can only be sustained by the same kind of selective reading and partial blindness that has allowed him to be portrayed as pedophilic, socially paralyzed and terrified of adult women.

His diaries alone can show the simplistic absurdity of trying to confine him in the straitjacket of religious conformity. This is a man who visited theatres and read novels, despite such activities being outlawed by Tractarians like his own father; who openly visited the church of radical F. D. Maurice, and who, for undeclared reasons, risked losing his job rather than take his vows and become an ordained minister. This is also a man whose shelves were filled with books exploring alternative aspects of belief, from Theosophy to spiritualism.

How much he believed of any of these alternatives is not known, for Dodgson left very little record of his private views on these or any matters. And, as with other aspects of his life—most notably his relationships with women—he seems to have deliberately courted an ambiguous understanding of his religious outlook. Examples are legion, but here are just a few.

To an 'unidentified recipient', dated by Cohen in the published Letters as 'mid-1882' Dodgson wrote:

> My dear father was what is called a "High Churchman and I naturally adopted those views.... But I doubt I am fully a 'High Churchman' now....

But on 7 July 1885 he wrote to Jemima Rix (mother of Edith, one of his adult girl-friends):

> I myself belong to the 'High Church' school. My dear father was a 'High Church' man, though not a Ritualist, and I have seen little cause to modify the views I learned from him...."

In the same letter to Mrs Rix, he says:

> I would escort [Edith] with pleasure to (the door of) any place of worship she liked to attend! But I would not go in

[if it was Weseleyan, or Baptist, or 'Plymouth brethren']...I should not object to attending a Roman Catholic service. I have done so, when abroad...

This is technically true. He did attend Catholic services when abroad and protestant services weren't available—but did he approve of them? According to his friend Henry Liddon's diary for 2 September 1867 (during the visit they both paid to Russia):

Some discussion with Dodgson in the evening. He thought the Roman Catholic Church like a concert room and went out...

And what about his views on Ritualism, the most extreme 'catholic' wing of the Anglican Church? In Sylvie and Bruno Concluded [Preface, 1893] he acknowledges that Ritualism was:

sorely needed and ...has effected a vast improvement in our Church services", but had eventually "gone too far".

Yet in the 1882 letter to an 'unknown recipient' quoted above he claims

[I] have always felt repelled by the yet higher development of Ritualism

He thinks Ritualism was sorely needed but also repellant. He is a High Churchman who isn't High Church any more. He has visited Roman Catholic ceremonies when abroad, though he thought they were like a concert room and walked out.

How to reconcile these seemingly irreconcilable contradictions? I think the answer is to understand what purpose was served by writing them. Was he conveying the truth about himself, or permitting someone else to construct their own 'truth' by providing the raw materials needed? With that in mind let's look more closely at these statements:

> My dear father was what is called a "High Churchman" and I naturally adopted those views.... But I doubt I am fully a 'High Churchman' now...."

The all-important and open-ended qualifiers "doubt" and "fully" turn this apparently solid statement into a mist of allusiveness. 'I doubt I am fully a High Churchman now' can mean he has serious doubts about the basic nature of High Church doctrines, or it can mean he has some small and quite trivial differences that don't amount to anything very much, depending on where we choose to put the emphasis. In fact it tells us almost nothing about what Dodgson really thinks about High Church-ness at all. Likewise in his letter to the High Church Mrs Rix; wherein he seems to be telling her that he too has High Church sympathies, very little is as it might first appear..

> I myself belong to the 'High Church' school. My dear father was a 'High Church' man, though not a Ritualist, and I have seen little cause to modify the views I learned from him..."

"I have seen little cause to modify those views" can, just as "I doubt I am fully a High Church man now," mean different things to different people. How much is 'little'? And notice he doesn't say whether this 'little' cause (whatever it might be) actually did make him modify his views or not. Presumably, if he was being truthful in the first quotation ('I doubt I am fully a High Churchman now'), then he has indeed "modified" his views, but his careful use of language allows him to elide this uncomfortable fact when dealing with Mrs Rix, and to permit her to believe she is talking to a man who shares her High Church convictions—*even though he never says any such thing*. As with the previous example he constructs in that slight sentence a kind of blank space wherein anyone who reads it can place what they want or expect to find there. He makes us think we are seeing him, but in fact we are looking into a mirror.

This is why anyone who wants to write about Lewis Carroll needs first and foremost to recognise who they are dealing with. This man, so long filed away as a simple-hearted dreamer, was possibly one of the most subtle, elusive and tricksterish individuals of his time, and nowhere more so than when writing about himself and his inmost heart. He stands in his own self portrayals as something implied rather than stated. His use of language was generally to defend against being known rather than to elucidate himself. He vanishes like a magician behind a haze of smoke even while he seems superficially to be delivering himself into the hands of his readers. If you take him at his word—or only some of his words—you will be deceived, as he probably intended you should be, not by him, but by yourself. He offers biographers the easy prize of confirmation in a single cherry picked sentence. Like Mrs Rix they see what they wish to see and stop searching for anything more.

This is no doubt partially why the myths of his life have been so thickly accrued, so hard to chip away. Certainty is appealing to people, ambiguity not so. And no biographer likes to admit they've been tricked by their subject. But maybe thing really are changing now. This present book tries to look at some aspects of Lewis Carroll's philosophy and religion that lie well beyond the narrow little scope of the Myth. Of course it doesn't pretend to present the entire truth and th final word, but is probably all the closer to the curious, subtle infinitely variegated reality of Charles Dodgson for accepting that limitation.

Karoline Leach

Taunton, October 2012

Preface

The following pages are an attempt to explore what I consider to be "curiosities" in the children's literature of Lewis Carroll. My quest to unearth the philosophical underpinnings of the *Alice* and *Looking-Glass* books has had a thirty-three year gestation. I was a graduate student in Philosophy when, for pleasure, I read *Alice's Adventures in Wonderland* and *Through the Looking-Glass*. The juxtaposition of the *Alice* books with my graduate work raised some questions. Was there something "vaguely philosophical" about the books? Had Carroll hidden other messages behind the frivolity of hookah-smoking caterpillars? Time and circumstances weren't right in 1973 for me to investigate the problem, but I never stopped wondering about it. Thirty-three years later, the time was right to ask the questions in a serious and scholarly way. This book is the result of that question asking. Although it represents serious scholarship, it is also intended to be fun. Parts of it were written with tongue so in cheek that Lewis Carroll himself might well have chuckled! The scholarship is softly mixed with the kind of academic frivolity that Carroll would have enjoyed... while pointedly directing the reader to Carroll's vibrant, intentional intellectual spirituality.

The past several years have seen a concentrated move by some newer Carrollian scholars to position Carroll in the theological and philosophical context of his time.[1] This work has had the effect of deconstructing numerous myths that have been, hitherto, unquestioned. My contribution to this movement focuses on the *Alice* and *Sylvie and Bruno* books, looking for suggestions of philosophical content. In doing so, I found, as expected, satirizations and allegorical treatments of several mid-nineteenth century theories of knowledge. My findings, however, went far beyond these initial expectations. I had expected to find Carroll reacting to an advancing tide of empiricism, and I did. I did not, however, expect his reaction to take on the particular shape or substance that it did. My preliminary expectations had been that his reactions would be more conservative and traditional. Where I thought that I would find a mathematically based position, I found, instead, a radical religio-philosophical counter-response to patriarchal materialism. To borrow from contemporary jargon, Carroll's personal epistemology took on a *counter-cultural flavour* as he battled to come to grips with the scope and limits of material existence. His intellectual journey, intentionally or otherwise, carried him deep into the waters of mysticism. Nineteenth century currents of spiritualism, theosophy and occult philosophy co-mingled with Carroll's interest in revived Platonism and Neoplatonism. The image of Carroll as a dreary Victorian conservative gave way to that of a man with wide intellectual parameters, an inquiring mind and bold, far-sighted vision. The work, essentially, offers yet another perspective toward the ongoing, contemporary deconstruction

---

1 Most notably, among these scholars, are Pascale Renaud-Grosbras, Hugues Lebailly, Karoline Leach, John Tufail, Mike Leach, and Jenny Woolf.

of the Carroll Myth. I am interested in both the man behind the myth… and the myths behind the man. Through rigorous philosophical recontextualization, I have attempted to demonstrate that myth, in its most primary sense, was as essential to the de-mythologized Lewis Carroll as it was to Plato.

It is worth noting that every chapter title, as well as that of the book itself, incorporates the word *behind*. This reflects Carroll's deliberation between the words *behind* and *through* when he named his second *Alice* book. Initially, the book was named *Behind the Looking-Glass* until Carroll opted to implement John Ruskin's suggestion of changing the word to *through*. Since this point is significant in viewing Carroll's system of ideas, I carried the theme through the chapter titles. The reader should note that whereas the *Alice* books are well-crafted literature, containing philosophical allegory, the *Sylvie and Bruno* books are notably more forthright, with an agenda that is quite obvious, though positioned in a weaker literary vessel.

Charles Lutwidge Dodgson, turned Lewis Carroll, exemplified the imperatives of Romantic introspection. He sketched and drew, photographed, wrote, sought beauty in nature, lectured in mathematics and logic, was passionate about theatre, was an inquiring theologian and open-mindedly investigated a wide range of phenomenal possibilities. The *Alice* and *Sylvie and Bruno* books provided a unique point of conjunction between his intellect and spirituality. Having lost belief in the theological and mythological master plots of earlier eras, Carroll turned his instinctive hunger for cosmic coherence and existential order toward the imaginative fiction of wonderlands rife with philosophical content.

Sherry L. Ackerman
Mount Shasta, 2012

Acknowledgements

$\mathcal{S}$pecial acknowledgements are given to the three Philosopher Kings to whom I have dedicated the book. The late Dr Foster "Scotty" Tait, Professor *Emeritus*, University of South Carolina, was really the inspiration for the book. He lit the flame of inquiry and turned my raw passion for philosophy into a systematic, rigorous search for meaning. I am forever indebted to his insistence upon scholarly discourse, critical methodology and creative visioning. Dr Robert McKay, Professor of Philosophy, Norwich University, demonstrated the patience of a monk as he read seemingly endless drafts and rewrites of the manuscript. His input was invaluable and substantially shaped the direction of the book. There are so many places in the text where his critique deepened the inquiry and opened possibilities. Dr Daniel Kealey, Professor *Emeritus*, Towson University, fuelled the flames and kept my enthusiasm alive through cold, dark winter nights of writing. He served as editor to the manuscript, and I am especially indebted to his meticulous attention to grammatical detail. I also wish to acknowledge my daughter, Jec A. Ballou and son, Christopher C. Ballou, who were uncomplainingly neglected as Alice became my constant companion. They, somehow, became accustomed to having stacks of books, instead of dinner, on the table more times than not.

I would like to thank Nancy C. Gerth for producing the index to the first edition.

And, finally, I am grateful to Charles Lutwidge Dodgson, turned Lewis Carroll, for his incredibly productive intellect. The legacy he left the world is impressive and I, for one, have been deeply enriched by it.

Introduction

In practical terms, ultimate unification with the divine can be described as a surrendered egoless state in which the external world synchronizes with the mystic's true nature and purpose.[2]

When Oxford mathematical lecturer Charles Lutwidge Dodgson made the metamorphosis into Lewis Carroll, it is unlikely that he had any idea that his *Alice* books would become literary classics. For children who had been confined to the dreary conventionality of Victorian existence, the sweep of his imagination opened the door to a new and fanciful world. Yet, a century-plus after their release, *Alice's Adventures in Wonderland* and *Through the Looking-Glass* still provide playful escape from everyday cares for both children and adults. There is, however, an element in Carroll's imaginative literature that goes beyond mere fantasy—an element that, in Alice's words, is "curiouser and curiouser!"

In a broad sense, the story of philosophical inquiry in England is a history of the changes in view of the structure and foundations of knowledge. When, as a result of the birth

---

2 Evelyn Underhill, *Mysticism* (New York: E. P. Dutton & Co., Inc., 1911), p. 71.

of the new sciences, the men of the seventeenth century lost faith in the innate capabilities of the mind, a gradual shift from rationalism toward empiricism took place. The two positions, though fundamentally opposed, were not always mutually exclusive and clear parameters for each were often difficult to define.

The early eighteenth century was dominated by the idea that man, nature and even deity could be explained by Newtonian physics. The validity and reliability of claims to knowledge of the external world through sense perception, as well as the propriety of claims to knowledge beyond the limits of sense perception, were challenged in the attempts to construct a sound theory of knowledge. This conception of natural philosophy, as a body of knowledge based firmly on experienced facts or experiment and observation, had sprung from the scholastic tradition of the thirteenth century, when Albertus Magnum and Aquinas had grafted Aristotle's natural philosophy onto Christian theology. Natural philosophy's emphasis on a body of knowledge based on observation and experimentation prepared the way for the empirical principles of the seventeenth century. Further advocacy for the emerging empirical paradigm was supplied by the widespread popularity of John Locke's *Essay Concerning Human Understanding.*

During this period, Plato had few partisans who were courageous enough to defend him against the ground swell of empiricism. However, in the second half of the eighteenth century there began to be a strong revival of interest in Platonism and Neoplatonism as a result of the earlier influence of the Cambridge School (c.1650–1700), and the work of Thomas Taylor, the Platonist (1758–1835). The influence that the Cambridge School had on the Platonic Renaissance in England cannot be underestimated. Without sympathy, the Cambridge School opposed the advance of science as founded by Galileo and Kepler, since this School saw it as the forerunner of a mechanistic view of nature that violated their ethical and spiritual convictions. The Cambridge Platonists looked upon themselves as the guardians of a religious and philosophical tradition that they attempted to trace, fortify and defend by a thorough acquaintance with, and interpretation of, its sources. In this sense, they were trying to construct an invulnerable foundation for a metaphysical spiritualism. In the history of English philosophy, empiricism occupied the focus of attention and the Cambridge School was "granted an historical significance only in so far as it had co-operated, as rival and adversary, in the formation of the empirical philosophy, and produced in it certain polemical reactions."[3] However, the real intellectual principles that Cambridge Platonism stood for bound it to the past through the philosophical movement of the Italian and English Renaissance, and to the future in the general history of thought for ensuing centuries.

Albeit the Cambridge Platonists appeal to and venerate Plato, their achievements were by no means the direct continuation of Platonic thought. Many essential phases of Platonism never enter into their view, while other features of the thought are so greatly modified that they are scarcely recognizable. "In these writers the teachings of Plato always appear as if they were transformed through a refracting medium."[4] The Cambridge Circle drew heavily upon the interpretation of Platonic philosophy offered by Marsilio Ficino and the Florentine Academy. For Cudworth and More,[5] as for Ficino[6] and Pico della Mirandola,[7] Plato formed a link in the golden chain of divine revelation. Plato, the ancestor and patron of the *philosophia perennis*,[8] was for them

---

3   Ernst Cassirer, *The Platonic Renaissance in England,* trans. James P. Pettegrove (Austin: University of Texas Press, 1953), 4.
4   Ibid., 8.
5   The Cambridge Platonists were a group of English seventeenth-

the living proof that true philosophy is never opposed to genuine theology.

In 1881, Thomas M. Johnson wrote an article, *The Way and the Wisdom Teachers,* for *The Platonist, I* in which he traced the gradual progression from Platonic idealism toward nineteenth century England's interest in theosophy and spiritualism. He cited that reactions created by the cold, barren dogmas of modern science had served as catalysts for a revival in the mystical beliefs of Platonism, Neoplatonism and Pythagoreanism. Johnson's reference would certainly have included the work of Thomas Taylor, the Platonist. Taylor continued along the lines initiated by the Cambridge School in his denunciation of eighteenth century deism as "the experimental farrago of the moderns" and declared that "the long lost philosophy of Pythagoras and Plato" were infinitely superior to it.[9] He further asserted that Plato was the greatest link in a chain of transmitters of a philosophy first promulgated by Orpheus, then by Pythagoras. Plato, according to Taylor, concealed in obscurity from the vulgar

century thinkers associated with the University of Cambridge. The most important philosophers among them were Ralph Cudworth (1617-1689) and Henry More (1614-1687).

6 Marsilio Ficino (1433-1499), the Florentine, was a man who wrought a deep and lasting change in European society. From him and his Academy, the Renaissance drew its most potent intellectual and spiritual inspiration. To Ficino, the writings of Plato and his followers contained the key to the most important knowledge for man: knowledge of him/herself, that is, knowledge of the divine and immortal principle within him/her. See Plato, *Timaeus,* 41; *Phaedrus,* 245c-246a.

7 Pico della Mirandola (1463-1494), an Italian Neoplatonist and student of Marsilio Ficino, who was interested in positing a reconciliation between religion and philosophy.

8 For an excellent resource on the *philosophia perennis,* see *The Perennial Philosophy,* by Aldous Huxley (New York and London: Harper & Brothers Publishers, 1945).

and ignorant the most sublime of his doctrines. These were the teachings, in short, of the ancient mystery schools. The meanings lay hidden for years until the appearance of the Alexandrians. Men such as Plotinus, Porphyry, Iamblichus, Syriacus, Proclus, Hierocles, Sallust and Damascius freed the mystical doctrines of Plato from obscurity. Taylor's interpretations of the ancient doctrines fuelled the interest in ancient mystery teachings that was growing in nineteenth century England. Evidence of this influence was being seen in the Romantics' emphasis on the truths buried in literary symbol, allegory and myth. Many of the poets, writers and artists of this period held that Plato and his followers concealed divine truths in allegory and ambiguity. Several of the Romantics, among the most prominent of whom is Blake, not only accounted for the enigmas in the writing of the ancients by the doctrine of intentional obscurity, but accepted it as a fundamental aesthetic principal in their own work.

In addition to the Cambridge School and Taylor's interpretations, Plato's teachings had also undergone other modifications and transmutations that had inevitably occurred as they had filtered through the various perspectives of the subsequent schools. Some philosophical elements that formed Middle Platonism, the period between the Old Academy and the Neoplatonists, had become primary components of Gnosticism. Although Gnosticism emerged as a set of transformations belonging to a multidimensional, variable system, there were two criteria that were generally found. One was the criterion of *ecosystemic intelligence,* which is the degree to which the universe can be attributed to an intelligent and good cause. The other criterion was the *anthropic principle,* which is the affirmation of the commensurability and mutual link between human beings and the universe at

---

9   George Mills Harper, *The Neoplatonism of William Blake* (Chapel Hill: University of North Carolina Press, 1961), 11.

large.[10] The basic Gnostic myth is that the creator described in Genesis is not the true god, but an inferior Demiurge. The Demiurge has many ministers, or archons, and together they are responsible for the miserable world. Though imprisoned in matter, humanity carries within itself the leftover sparks of the Pleroma (Fullness) that existed before the Demiurge and his creation. Our bodies and souls cloak this spiritual spark and must be rent for us to discover our true being.

The corpus of Greek writings attributed to Hermes Trismegistus and often quoted as the *Poimandres* is also regarded as a prime document of independent pagan Gnosticism. Therefore, concurrent with Victorian England's revival of interest in Platonic and Neoplatonic thought, we see a resurgence of Gnostic themes in literature from the period. To the poet, writer or artist of Romantic or mystical temperament, Neoplatonism and Gnosticism walked hand-in-hand, teaching that there is a realm of Beauty beyond the sensible world which is perceptible to the mind. Carroll's own Christ Church colleague, J. A. Stewart, in *Platonism in English Poetry,* wrote:

> Platonism, I would describe, in the most general terms, as the mood of one who has a curious eye for the endless variety of this visible and temporal world and a fine sense of its beauties, yet is haunted by the presence of an invisible and eternal world behind, or, when the mood is most pressing, within, the visible and temporal world, and sustaining both it and himself—a world not perceived as external to himself, but inwardly, lived by him, as that with which, at moments of ecstasy, or even habitually, he is become One.[11]

---

10 Ioan P. Couliano, *The Tree of Gnosis: Gnostic Mythology from Early Christianity to Modern Nihilism* (San Francisco: Harper Collins, 1992), 71.

The substantive teachings of the ancient Greek mystery schools were reinforced in nineteenth century England through the growing popularity of the Theosophical Movement. Theosophical teachings connected the dots between ancient mystery schools and nineteenth century fraternal orders.[12] An article from *Theosophy*, dated March 5, 1939, asks "how many realize that *no initiated* philosopher had the right to reveal his knowledge clearly, but was obliged by the law of the sanctuary to conceal the truth under the veil of allegory or symbol?" Roger Bacon, centuries earlier, in *Wisdom of Keeping Secrets* (c.1260), had similarly written, "a man is crazy who writes a secret unless he conceals it from a crowd and leaves it so that it can be understood only by effort of the studious and wise." Lewis Carroll was not a crazy man... and he did a masterful job of concealing his secrets from the crowd.

---

11 John Gregory, *The Neoplatonists* (London: Kyle Cathie Ltd., 1991), 249.

12 *Theosophy*, Vol. 27, No. 4, February, 1939

Contents

PART I

Lewis Carroll

CHAPTER I

The Myths behind the Maker

Ever drifting down the stream—
Lingering in the golden gleam—
Life, what is it but a dream?
Through the Looking-Glass

> Is all our Life, then, but a dream
> Seen faintly in the golden gleam
> Athwart Time's dark resistless stream?
> *Sylvie and Bruno*

The world is but a Thought, said he:
The vast unfathomable sea
Is but a Notion—unto me.
Rhyme? And Reason?

The one constant pertaining to mythic characters is that their life stories transcend objectivity. Whether we take as our example Dionysus, Persephone... or Lewis Carroll... the fact remains that historical impressions are dominated by subjective claims to truth. Biographies of Carroll conspicuously lack consensus in their attempts to construct an objective biographical persona.[13] The essence of myth is exemplified in these conflicting accounts. Myth doesn't exist objectively apart from the myth-makers and, as such, represents a subjective relationship between the story teller and an archetype. This being so, we might be well advised to look at Carroll from an archetypal, as opposed to purely biographical, perspective. In choosing this lens, my claims regarding Carroll should be considered from the basis of coherence,[14] rather than correspondence,[15] theory.

What might be found in the content of an archetypal nineteenth-century Romantic? In short... a life exemplifying the Platonic imperative toward The Good, The Beautiful and The True. Platonism, well stirred into a mix of Neoplatonism and Pythagoreanism, represented one of the central currents of the intellectual climate in nineteenth-century England. In the Allegory of the Cave,[16] Plato offered an insight into why philosophers have the possibility to attain happiness, whereas non-philosophers do not. Non-philosophers are like the prisoners in the cave, content to believe that mere images are reality. The philosopher leaves the cave and moves beyond the images of things to things themselves, then onto the world of the Forms and, finally, to The Good itself. The myth ends with the philosopher returning to the cave in an attempt to enlighten his fellow prisoners. It could be said that Lewis Carroll both left, and returned, to the cave. Drawing, sketching, and photographing images moved him toward things themselves. Long walks in the countryside, afternoon

---

13 See *In the Shadow of the Dreamchild: A New Understanding of Lewis Carroll*, by Karoline Leach (London: Peter Owens Publishing, 1999).

14 A coherence theory of truth states that the truth of any proposition consists in its coherence with some specified set of propositions.

15 A correspondence theory of truth states that the truth conditions of propositions are objective features in the world.

16 Plato, *Republic*, 514a-515b.

tea parties with children, *a priori* mathematical and logical truths revealed things themselves, forming a springboard into the world of The Forms. We see this principle illustrated in the Cult of Childhood that was glorified in so much of the literature and art of the Victorian period. The adoration of children as good, innocent and in some way connected with spirituality, had been reintroduced from the Orphic theogony into British Romanticism. It could, thus, be suggested that Lewis Carroll's return to the cave, playing on the Cult of Childhood, was a deliberate attempt to enlighten the imprisoned through his carefully crafted stories of liberation.

The Platonic dialogues are rich in discussions of The Beautiful. In the *Symposium*,[17] for example, Plato presents a progression toward The Beautiful, outlining five distinct stages of ascent, as follows:

(1) It is the longing for what one lacks that propels one through the ascent. Since we exist in the sensible world, we begin by being attracted to a beautiful body. We eventually realize that the very thing which makes this particular body beautiful is found in all beautiful bodies.

(2) One then comes to realize that a beautiful soul is even more lovely than a beautiful body, causing one to love all beautiful souls, even if they are in unattractive bodies.

(3) This leads one to contemplate the beauty of a harmonious social order, since beautiful souls can only blossom in orderly and just political communities.

(4) One then moves to the realm of the sciences, which provide the foundations for the harmonious social order—a social order founded upon true knowledge (*episteme*) rather than mere opinion (*doxa*).

(5) The final stage of our ascent is impossible to explain to those who have not experienced it themselves. It can be described as the mystical vision of The Beautiful, which for Plato, as we shall see a bit later on, is actually the same as The Good. This

---

17 Plato, *Symposium*, 210a-211b.

experience, which is described in ecstatic language, comes close to the mystical vision of God described by Christian authors in the Middle Ages. Unlike the other kinds of beauty that we have seen, the vision of The Beautiful is a glimpse of something transcendent and eternal and causes delight in those who experience it.

Plato maintained that all human beings long to possess The Beautiful/Good, for it is the very nature of our being to seek Truth. If we are satisfied to be confined to material reality, we will never be fulfilled. It is incumbent upon those who have attained the vision of The Beautiful/Good to lead us beyond the material realm into the realm of The Forms. Carroll found himself in the intellectual storm-center of England. Materialism was gaining ground at Oxford. The Commissioner's Report on Educational Reform at Oxford (April 1852) emphatically demanded that science should receive fair play. Traditional theological issues took a back seat to a wider variety of philosophical concerns in College Common Room discussions. Mark Pattison was said to have boasted that "German philosophy superceded the Fathers."[18] The Ashmolean museum was a visible sign that clerical Oxford had opened her gates to the advancing tide of science. Many Oxford dons were apprehensive that this tide might diffuse the value of philosophy, history, language and religion. Thomas Hill Green, erstwhile, was making his powers felt, in his teachings of philosophy at Balliol, as an example of the thoughtful liberals of the era. Another corruptive catalyst was the empiricist philosophy of John Stuart Mill, whose works attained enormous prestige at Cambridge and throughout England. The dominant theme of Mills *Logic* (1843) was that the only legitimate source of information man had about the

---

18 Charles Edward Mallet, *A History of the University of Oxford (18th and 19th Centuries)*, vol. 3 (London: Methuen Co., Ltd, 1927), 354.

world was the physical senses; conversely, faith was not a valid foundation for belief.

The clash between the advancing tide of empiricism and the old traditional values of the High Church came to a climax with the *Essays and Reviews* controversy. The failure of many Anglican hierarchy to repudiate the higher critics and radical freethinkers scandalized the Evangelicals, whose outraged response was considered reactionary by the scholarly community. In 1861, *Essays and Reviews*, co-authored by Jowett, Pattison, Baden-Powell, Temple and Goodwin, expressed alarm lest, "the majority of Churchmen, by holding fast the narrow, fundamental beliefs, should estrange themselves more and more from contemporary thought."[19] In this volume the Essayists allegorized their theological position by stating that if a ship's company were to claim that they had seen a mermaid, surely no-one would believe them. Whereas, if this same company were to claim that they saw something that they believed to be a mermaid, it would be easily conceded. Mark Pattison cited this example in urging Churchmen to allow supremacy of reason to prevail through all religious thinking. Jowett maintained, "Scripture must be interpreted like any other book...."[20] Oxford, the English Church and the country as a whole were fiercely divided on the question of reason versus doctrine.

At this time, Archdeacon Wilberforce offered a counter-position to *Essays and Reviews* in his *Replies to Essays and Reviews*. In the preface he denounced the rationalist movement as a "daring claim for the unassisted human intellect to be able to measure and explain all things." Lewis Carroll

---

19 Alfred William Benn, *The History of English Rationalism in the Nineteenth Century*, vol. 1 (London: Longmans, Green, and Co., 1906), 3.

20 Alan Gauld, *The Founders of Psychical Research* (London: Routledge & K. Paul, 1968), 49.

shared the Archdeacon's position. Carroll's study of mathematics had convinced him that there were limits to the human intellect. We find evidence of Carroll's position on the faculty of human reason in a letter that he wrote to Daniel Biddle, mathematical editor of the *Educational Times*. In the letter, Carroll interprets Zeno's second paradox as the response to Biddle's question involving infinite regress of ever-diminishing distances. Carroll states that we cannot conceive how a point, moving from "0" to "1", through an infinite series of steps, ever reaches "1", but that a thing is not impossible merely because it is inconceivable.[21] The limitations of human reason do, thus, not limit the possibility of the reality of unknown phenomenon.

The already frail faith of many in the established Church was further eroded by the publication of Charles Darwin's *Origin of Species* (1859). The time was ripe for great collisions of principles and aims. Just as Archdeacon Wilberforce had been outspoken in a reply to the Essayists, legend has it that he also agreed to debate Thomas Henry Huxley over Darwin's claims that man descended from "ape, as opposed to angel." The apparent debate that ensued between Wilberforce and Huxley (1860) gave the superficial impression of being about doctrinal issues. However, it is just as likely that Wilberforce's primary incentive in attacking Darwin's theory, as it had been in countering the Essayists, was to refute materialism. The proponents of self-evident truths and *a priori* knowledge were faced with evaluating and determining the causes for religion, and of the issues raised by these debates. Theology had ceased in its supreme reign, but the instincts that produced it had not ceased to stir inquiry. Carroll allied with Wilberforce in his position on both the Essayists and the Evolutionists. It

---

21 Morton N. Cohen and Roger Lancelyn Green, eds. *The Letters of Lewis Carroll*: vol. 1 (New York: Oxford University Press, 1979), 589.

has been noted that Carroll could not mention Darwin without bitterness. After endeavouring to arrive at some conclusions as to the message of the Christian doctrines from the expositions of contemporary scholars and theologians, forever in dispute with one another, Carroll found himself outside the rigidly Anglican system.[22] Carroll, like the Wilberforces, had become interested in immaterial phenomenon and direct spiritual experience (*gnosis*).

Both Carroll and the Wilberforces, albeit Anglican clergymen, were active participants in the theosophical movement that was spreading through Victorian England. Basil Wilberforce made his theosophical interests public with the publication of *Mystic Immanence*, in which he stated that the essence of the ancient gnosis was the oneness of the human soul with the Universal Soul.[23] Carroll's theosophical and spiritualist interests are documented though his membership in the Society for Psychical Research and the Ashmolean Society, as well as in his private library holdings. Alan Gauld, author of *The Founders of Psychical Research*, estimated that, in England, by the 1860s and 70s, "... the existence of four fairly successful periodicals suggest that the number of active Spiritualists must have been well into five figures. The numbers of those influenced by Spiritualism, or at least interested in it, may have been perhaps ten times greater.[24] The Society for Psychical Research was founded in February 1882 and Charles Lutwidge Dodgson's name appears in the charter list of members, along with William Gladstone, Arthur Balfour, Alfred Tennyson and John Ruskin, dated 1883. Further, at the time of Carroll's death, numerous books on

---

22 Although Dodgson/Carroll had served as an Anglican Deacon, it is notable that he declined to proceed to Holy Orders.

23 William Kingsley, *The Gnosis or Ancient Wisdom in the Christian Scriptures* (London: George Allen and Unwin Ltd., 1937), 57.

24 Gauld, *Founders of Psychical Research,* 77.

the subject were listed in the estate catalogue including Home's *Lights and Shadows of Spiritualism*, Thomson's *Philosophy of Magic*, Christmas' *Phantom World* and numerous books on the occult, among which was Gilchrist's *Life of William Blake*.[25] Further evidence of Carroll's theosophical associations are found in the documentation that he lectured to a meeting of the Ashmolean Society (November 1860) on the topic "Where does the day begin?"[26] The Ashmolean Society was founded by Elias Ashmole, an English mystic, for the purposes of reconstructing ancient Platonic and Gnostic mysticism.[27]

The foundation for a modern Spiritualist movement had been put in place through the enterprises of three eccentrics. Emanuel Swedenborg, a Swedish engineer turned prophet, who communicated with angels and spirits, had published *Arcana Coelestia* in London in 1749; Franz Mesmer, an Austrian physician branded unacceptable by the world of learning, popularized the idea of trance and the concept of animal magnetism (c. 1775), and Andrew Jackson Davis, a young American good-for-nothing who took to seeing visions, became the first theorist of the Spiritualist movement through the publication in 1847 of his channeled work, *The Principles of Nature, Her Divine Revelations*.[28] The crisis of consciousness that overtook nineteenth century England could be likened to the cultural adjustment of the Renaissance period.

---

25 Alexander L. Taylor, *The White Knight: A Study of C.L. Dodgson (Lewis Carroll)* (Philadelphia: Dufour Editions, 1963), 179.

26 Stuart Dodgson Collingwood, *Life and Letters of Lewis Carroll* (New York: The Century Co., 1898), 85.

27 Manly P. Hall, *Lectures on Ancient Philosophy: An Introduction to the Study and Application of Rational Procedure* (Los Angeles: The Hall Publishing Co., 1929), 411.

28 James Webb, *The Occult Underground*, (Peru, Illinois: Open Court Publishing Co., 1974), 21-26.

> What was happening was the final collapse of the old world-order
> which had first been rudely assaulted during the Renaissance and
> Reformation... just when the Age of Reason seemed to be bearing
> fruit in the nineteenth century, there was an unexpected reaction
> against the very method which brought success, a wild return to
> archaic forms of belief, and among the intelligentsia a sinister
> concentration on superstitions which had been thought
> buried....[29]

Bereft of assurances of immortality after so great an attack on biblical revelation were masses of hopeless people begging for a revelation that was scientifically demonstrable. Ensuing was a widespread flight from reason and a revival of occult traditions that had been discredited in the Enlightenment.

Interestingly, the original version of *Alice,* begun in 1862, did not contain the Cheshire-Cat, the Pig and Pepper, or the Mad Tea-Party, and contained only a very abbreviated trial of the Knave of Hearts. These additions occurred during the re-working of the manuscript, between 1862 to 1865, while Oxford, the English Church and the country as a whole were fiercely divided on the religio-philosophical questions of doctrine versus reason. During this period, Carroll read Charles Kingsley's *Water Babies* and found all of the questions of the day "neatly wrapped up," as Kingsley said, in allegory and satire.[30] Considerations of evolution, spiritualism and materialism were set into the enlivened "nonsense" of *Water Babies,* and probably encouraged Carroll to introduce more allegory and satire into his developing *Alice* manuscript.

There are a number of similarities between Carroll's works and Kingsley's *Water Babies.* Notably, both authors allegorize problems of perception and their subsequent moral implications. Kingsley and Carroll were both interested in psychic research and its implications for perception. Carroll,

29 Ibid., 7-8.
30 Taylor, *White Knight,* 53.

in fact, makes a direct reference to this in the Introduction to *Sylvie and Bruno Concluded.* In the period from 1868 to 1876, Carroll's interest in psychic research escalated. In a letter to James Langton Clarke (December 4, 1882) Carroll wrote:

> I have just read a small pamphlet, the first report of the Psychical Society, on 'thought-reading.' The evidence, which seems to have been most carefully taken... seems to point to the existence of a natural force, allied to electricity and nerve-force, by which brain can act on brain. I think we are close on the day when this shall be classed among the known natural forces, and its laws tabulated, and when the scientific skeptics, who always shut their eyes, till the last moment, to any evidence that seems to point beyond materialism, will have to accept it as a proven fact in nature.[31]

Here, it appears that Carroll is entertaining the epistemological question of whether of not it is possible to receive impressions from the mind of an agent by some means other than the ordinary senses. This line of inquiry is extended to ask if those impressions are received, on the other hand, from slight sensory indications unintentionally and unconsciously conveyed to them by the agent. While Carroll admittedly recognized a standard of normal perception, he also allowed that the acuteness with which different individuals perceive sensation could certainly pass through a wide scale of variation. For example, while one person may not be able to distinguish even primary colours, there are tribal weavers in Eastern Asia who can distinguish with certainty over three-hundred shades of a single colour which are entirely indistinguishable to ordinary Western eyes.[32] This idea gives objective reality to an immense body of knowledge

31 Cohen and Green, *Letters,* vol. 1, 471-2.
32 R. Osgood Mason, *Telepathy and the Subliminal Self* (New York: Henry Holt and Co., 1899), 74.

that is contrary to materialism. In this case, we find an example where ordinary sensory experience is unsatisfactory for providing consistently reliable public perceptions. To alleviate this problem, Carroll might have suggested that the methods for obtaining knowledge be broadened to include gnosis, or the experience of Pure Thought. The possibility for this sentiment is suggested in Carroll's *Rhyme and Reason:*

> "The world is but a Thought", said he:
> The vast unfathomable sea
> Is but a Notion—unto me.

In this passage, "Thought" is assigned a capital "T," a mystical short-hand for referencing the product of Universal Mind. The position is developed further when he continues:

> Thought in the mind doth still abide:
> That is by Intellect supplied,
> And within that Idea doth hide:
> And he, that yearns the truth to know,
> Still further inwardly may go,
> And find Idea from Notion flow:
> And thus the chain, that sages wrought
> For Notion hath its source in Thought.

Here, "Thought," "Intellect" and "Idea" are all capitalized, again suggesting that he is alluding to Universal Principles. Likewise, the verse continues, "Notion hath its source in Thought," indicating that even what appear to be our individual, or particular, notions are a part of Source. "Thought in the mind doth still abide: That is by Intellect supplied, And within that Idea doth hide," gives credence to gnosis. Carroll hints that the Idea is already present in the Intellect, dormant, waiting to be awakened by Thought. "And he, that yearns to know the truth, Still further inwardly may go," suggests that truth can be found by taking the inward journey of the mystic. Carroll strengthens this suggestion in the next line as he states, "And find Idea from Notion flow." Whereas a "notion" is a whim or fancy of the mind, while an "idea" is a more clearly defined image existing in the mind; the capitalization of both words intimates that Carroll is signifying that they are not particular, but Universal, qualities. Thus, an Idea can be arrived at by a process initiated by considering, or contemplating, the Notion. Carroll goes on to assert, "And thus the chain, that sages sought, Is to a glorious circle wrought, For Notion has its source in Thought." In these verses, he introduces the Platonic concept of Thought as timeless and continuous, without beginning or end. Likewise, he implies Platonic dualism, as both Notion and Idea, participants in both the phenomenal and noumenal realms, initiate and conclude in Thought. Finally, his allegorical reference to Platonism, "…the chain, that sages sought," echoing Thomas Taylor's assertion that Plato was the greatest link in a chain of transmitters of a philosophy first promulgated by Orpheus, then by Pythagoras.[33]

The conceptual world of Platonism offered a viable alternative to the empiricism that was sweeping Victorian England. One of the distinguishing characteristics of Platonism was the concept of philosophical realism. *Realism* refers to the notion that all words denote objects that have independent existence apart from the mind that creates language. If a word exists, then something denoted by that word also exists. Abstractions, therefore, have reality outside of language and beyond their function as conveniences of human thought. What we are inclined to dismiss as the fallacy of conceptual reification—treating conceptual tools as though they were objectified things—is commonplace in Platonism, indeed, essential to its whole approach to thinking. Therefore,

33 Thomas Taylor, *A Dissertation on the Eleusinian and Bacchic Mysteries* (New York: J. W. Bouton, 1875), p. 47.

for example, just as there are things—Mad Hatters—that correspond to the words *Mad Hatter*, so there is a thing—*redness*—that corresponds to the word *red*.

A second essential and, to materialistic ways of thinking, extremely odd characteristic of a Platonic framework, is the notion that there are degrees of reality. From an empirical standpoint, something is either real or it is not. In Platonism, everything possesses some degree of reality, and that degree can range from almost complete non-being to full being, from the very minimum degree of reality that can be present for something to exist at all to complete reality. Different positions, in the hierarchy of reality, are assigned to different things. Further, what materialism is inclined to think of as the best candidates for the highest positions in the hierarchy of realities would, in fact, occupy the lower positions. Whereas the materialist would consider concrete objects as the most unquestionably real entities we confront, abstractions and invisible entities would be problematic. In Platonism, however, the presuppositions are reversed: disembodied abstractions possess the highest degree of reality; concrete, material objects have considerably less. *Mad Hatter-ness* is more real than a particular *Mad Hatter* that we might encounter in the phenomenal world. *Redness* is more real than any particular sense experience involving the seeing of *red* objects. Indeed, the particular *Mad Hatter* or the particular experience of *red* is real only to the extent to which it participates in *Mad Hatter-ness* or *redness*. Participation is bound up in still another important characteristic of Platonism, which is its insistent dualism.

Platonic frameworks draw a dividing line between the two realms of existence. One realm, the inferior of the two, is the material, physical world of sense experience. It is the phenomenal world, the world of objects, of the body and of immediate perception. The other, the superior of the two, is the world of the immaterial world of realities not accessible to the body's senses. It is the world known by intellect or spiritual sense, the noumenal world. The noumenal world contains the Universals. Although Platonism is decidedly dualistic in its vision of two realms, it is paradoxically monistic in its notions regarding the relationships among the highest entities existing in the noumenal realm of ideas. The Good, The True and The Beautiful are actually all one Universal, being apparently separated for the sake of the limited intellect and perceptual faculties of ordinary human beings. The Good is The True, which is The Beautiful. In this sense, The Good, The True, and The Beautiful are never dissonant because the Universals, being in fact one and the same, cannot be in conflict. The name given to the one encompassing Universal varies greatly. Sometimes it is called The One, sometimes The Absolute. Often, the expression The Good denotes both the partial, moral aspect of The One and The One Itself. In other words, all of the principal Universals resolve into The One.

Human nature combines a material element—the body and its senses— and a noumenal element—the mind and spirit. *Mind* in Platonism is far more inclusive an entity than merely the rational or intellectual component. *Mind* includes all that enables us to make contact with invisible realities, both within ourselves and outside ourselves. The material aspect of human nature is constructed out of phenomenal matter and is, therefore, subject to all of the limitations and liabilities of the phenomenal world. The noumenal aspect of human nature originates, of course, in the noumenal world and, therefore, participates in its power and excellence. Since, however, *Mind* is entrapped in a material container that is located within the phenomenal world at some distance from the noumenal— *exiled in a distant country* is a common metaphor—-its power and excellence are obscured and impaired. The consummation of this discipline, of this "homeward journey out of exile" is conceived of as a transformation of the soul of the human being.

Nineteenth century Platonists were influenced by the Italian Renaissance philosopher Nicholas Cusanus, who developed a rich and complex view of the universe and human knowledge. Among his most important and far-reaching ideas was the idea that mathematical knowledge was always absolutely certain knowledge. They were also heavily influenced by the Renaissance Neoplatonist Marsilio Ficino, who believed that the purpose of human life was contemplation. The ultimate goal of human life was to be reunited with God, at least in an intellectual sense. This goal, according to Ficino, was accomplished through contemplation (*theoria*). At first, the human mind removes itself from the outside, physical world, and thinks about abstract ideas concerning knowledge and the soul. As it rises in knowledge it eventually reaches a point where it can arrive at an unmediated vision of God itself. This last stage would occur only after death and the immortality that the soul would enjoy would be an eternity of this vision of God. From this idea, Ficino developed the concept that he called Platonic Love, which had significant implications during the Victorian Period in England. While Ficino believed that the human soul pursued contemplation more or less in isolation, he acknowledged that human beings were fundamentally social. When the spiritual relationship between God and the individual, sought through contemplation, is reproduced in a friendship or love with another person, that constitutes spiritual or Platonic Love. In other words, when the love and spiritual activity in a friendship mirrors the love for God, then the two individuals have attained the highest type of friendship that they can.

The two most influential aspects of Platonism and Neoplatonism for Lewis Carroll, as we shall see, were its emphasis on the priority and certainty of mathematics and

Ficino's doctrine of Platonic Love. As the concept of Platonic Love diffused Victorian England's artistic and intellectual circles, writers, poets, philosophers and artists began associating erotic love with spiritual bonds, as reflective of the relationship between individuals and God. Likewise, the Platonic argument that mathematics was a form of certain knowledge got expanded to the radical thesis that mathematics represented the divine ideas. This extreme position, accepted by the bulk of the Neoplatonists, eventually became the basis for a new form of science. Whereas science had historically been dominated by purely qualitative, empirical claims, the new view asserted that the physical world was fundamentally mathematical. Thus, knowledge of mathematics was a requisite for preliminary access to the divine mind.

From this perspective, Carroll would not have found complete compatibility with the doctrine, for example, of Francis Bacon.[34] Bacon sharply divided knowledge into Inspired Divinity and Philosophy. He based his division on the idea that all knowledge was ultimately derived from one of two sources. It could be "inspired by divine revelation" or it could "arise from our senses." Apart from revelation all human knowledge arose from the senses. Bacon could not reconcile with the concept of pure reason, and felt that such a method was like a spider making cobwebs out of its own substance. He objected to allowing consideration of theological issues in the study of natural philosophy. He was annoyed when philosophers, in searching for the causes of natural phenomena, would think in terms of divine purposes rather than more immediately in terms of other natural phenomena. Alluding to number mysticism and the Theory of Forms,

---

34 Bacon contended that the only knowledge of importance to man was empirically rooted in the natural world and that a clear system of scientific inquiry would assure man's mastery over the world.

Bacon mentions that Pythagoras and Plato mistakenly felt that natural science had its basis in revelation.[35] Bacon's sharp mandatory division between philosophy and theology was diametrically opposed to Platonism and, as such, received a share of Carroll's satire.

Carrollian satire was also targeted at Berkeley's *New Theory of Vision* (1709) and Newman's *Tract XC* (1841), both of which questioned the validity of Euclidean geometry. In *Tract XC*, Newman found a weakness in the Thirty-Nine Articles and in the whole fabric on which the mathematical orthodoxy of the nineteenth century had been founded. "The truth is," he wrote, "we do not at all know what is meant by distance or intervals absolutely any more than we know what is meant by absolute time."[36] Berkeley, earlier, had laid the foundation for Newman's view by stating that an intelligence, with a sense of vision but no sense of touch, would be unable to imagine a solid object, or prove the congruence of triangles, or even imagine a plane figure, since this would require the idea of distance.

Such forthright empiricism took a sceptical view of the possibility of there being any metaphysical properties assigned to The Five Platonic Solids. Although the tetrahedron, octahedron, cube, icosahedron, and the dodecahedron had been known since ancient times, the first thorough examination of them is probably the *Theaetetus*. It is likely that Euclid learned the geometry of Theaetetus, with which he demonstrated familiarity, when he studied in Plato's Academy in Athens. It has been suggested that Euclid's *Elements* were originally written, not as a general treatise on geometry, but as a means to supply the necessary steps for a full

---

35 R. S. Woolhouse, *The Empiricists* (Oxford: Oxford University Press, 1988), 16.

36 J. H. Newman, *Tract XC: On Certain Passages in the XXXIX Articles* (London: Rivingtons, 1865), 47.

appreciation of the five regular solids.[37] Metaphysically minded Greeks associated the regular polyhedra with the four Elements and the Universe. Kepler's *Opera Omnia,* published in Frankfort in 1864, justified this correspondence by stating that the tetrahedron, having the smallest volume for its surface, and the icosahedron, having the largest, exhibit the qualities of dryness and wetness, and, therefore, correspond to Fire and Water. The cube, standing firmly on its own base, corresponds to the stable Earth, while the octahedron, which rotates freely when held by two opposite corners, corresponds to the mobile Air. Finally, the dodecahedron corresponds to the Universe, because the zodiac has twelve signs.[38] Kepler, although a forerunner of the scientific worldview, was nonetheless impelled by Neoplatonic motivations, having a passionate belief in the transcendent power of numbers and geometrical forms and a vision of the Sun as the central image of the Godhead, as well as being devoted to the celestial "harmony of the spheres." Writing to Galileo, Kepler invoked "Plato and Pythagoras, our true preceptors."[39]

For Carroll, the realm of possible knowledge was confined to neither the material nor the intellectual realm. The theosophical movement that swept through Victorian England proclaimed gnosis in the face of the prevailing agnosticism of the latter half of the nineteenth century. Annie Besant, in *The Ideals of Theosophy* (1912), summarized this sentiment as follows:

> Hard the sorrow and bitter the pain, wide the gulf and sore the passage: but it can be crossed by the man who realizes the Eternal, and who knows that nothing that earth can do can shake

---

37 W. W. Rouse Ball, *Mathematical Recreations and Essays* (London: MacMillan and Co., Ltd., 1892), 130.

38 Ibid., 132.

39 Richard Tarnas, *The Passion of the Western Mind* (New York: Ballantine Books, 1991), 256.

the serenity that is fixed on the rock of the Eternal. When death is conquered and life is his own, he rises in the plentitude of the Eternal Spirit, master of matter which has become his servant, in order that he may help humanity.[40]

Carroll's originally title for *Through the Looking-Glass,* was *Behind the Looking-Glass* but, after more deliberation, settled upon *Through.*[41] If we entertain the idea of Carroll employing the mirror as an ancient symbol for the earth and material existence, it becomes important as to whether Carroll takes his readers "through" or "behind" the looking glass. To go "behind" the mirror implies that we necessarily leave the material world of "mere shadows and reflections." The imperfect material world of reflections and the perfect world of the Forms are mutually exclusive. Platonic dualism mandates that an individual is either a prisoner in the cave or has achieved liberation. However, to go "through" the mirror implies that there is a progressive availability to this level of knowledge. This softer, inclusive concept allows one to peer "through" to the world of the Forms from the imperfect material world. Carroll attempted to have a mirror physically incorporated into the cover of Alice Liddell's personal copy of *Through the Looking-Glass,* but the idea proved impractical.[42]

Some very important comments on *Through the Looking-Glass* come from Alice Theodura Raikes, a remote connection of Carroll's by marriage. Sixty years after *Through the Looking-Glass* was published, Alice Raikes (then Mrs Wilson Fox) recalled a meeting that she and Carroll had shared in a garden:

---

40 Annie Besant, *The Ideals of Theosophy* (Adyan, Madras, India: The Theosophist's Office, 1912), 128.

41 Anne Clark Amor, *Lewis Carroll: A Biography* (London: Dent Publishing, 1979), 164.

42 Ibid., 168.

One day, hearing my name, he called me to him saying, 'So you are another Alice. I'm very fond of Alices. Would you like to come and see something which is very puzzling?' We followed him into the house which opened… upon the garden, into a room full of furniture with a tall mirror standing across one corner. 'Now', he said, giving me an orange, 'first tell me which hand you have got that in.' 'The right', I said. 'Now', he said, 'go and stand before that glass, and tell me which hand the little girl you see there has got it in.' After some perplexed contemplation, I said, 'The left hand.' 'Exactly', he said, 'and how do you explain that?' I couldn't explain it, but seeing that some solution was expected, I ventured, 'If I was on the other side of the glass, wouldn't the orange still be in my right hand?' I remember his laugh. 'Well done, little Alice', he said, 'the best answer I've had yet.'[43]

In her reply, young Alice Raikes affirms that the "other side of the glass" would provide a perception of the Form from which the imperfect copy in the material realm had been derived. In the perfect immaterial world on the other side of the glass, she would, of course, have the orange in her right hand as she knew it to be. The mirror, as a symbol of the material world, reversed what Alice Raikes knew to be true, and erroneously represented the orange as if it were in her left hand.

Dreams furnish another avenue to knowledge of the immaterial world and, therefore, offer another glimpse of life on the other side of the looking glass. In the final poem of *Through the Looking-Glass* Carroll suggests that material existence is merely a dream-state or illusionary reflection of another more real existence:

"Life, what is it but a dream?"

He repeats this question in *Sylvie and Bruno* when he writes:

---

43 Ibid., 174.

"Is all our Life, then, but a dream?"

Carroll builds on this idea by indicating how difficult it can often be to distinguish between the waking and dreaming states. In Chapter VIII of *Through the Looking-Glass* Carroll presents this difficulty:

> After a while the noise seemed gradually to die away, till all was dead silence, and Alice lifted up her head in some alarm. There was no one to be seen, and her first thought was that she must have been dreaming about the Lion and the Unicorn and those queer Anglo-Saxon Messengers. However, there was the great dish still lying at her feet, on which she had tried to cut the plum-cake, 'So I wasn't dreaming, after all', she said.

This difficulty in distinguishing the two states of consciousness presents a problem. When Alice exclaimed that "she didn't want to go among mad people," the Cheshire-Cat informed her that she couldn't help that, as "we're all mad here. I'm mad. You're mad." Compare the Cat's remarks with the following entry, of February 9, 1856, in Carroll's diary:

> Query: when we are dreaming and, as often happens, have a dim consciousness of the fact and try to wake, do we not say and do things which in waking life would be insane? May we not then sometimes define insanity as an inability to distinguish which is the waking and which is the sleeping life? We often dream without the least suspicion of unreality: 'Sleep hath its own world', and it is often as lifelike as the other.

This is a classic Platonic dilemma that is found, for example, in the *Theaetetus:*

> THEAETETUS: 'I certainly cannot undertake to argue that madmen or dreamers think truly, when they imagine, some of them that they are gods, and others that they can fly, and are flying in their sleep.'

SOCRATES: 'Do you see another question which can be raised about these phenomena, notably about dreaming and waking?'

THEAETETUS: 'What question?'

SOCRATES: 'A question which I think you must often have heard persons ask: how can you determine whether at this moment we are sleeping, and all our thoughts are a dream; or whether we are awake, and talking to one another in the waking state?'

THEAETETUS: 'Indeed, Socrates, I do not know how to prove the one any more than the other, for in both cases the facts precisely correspond; and there is no difficulty in supposing that during all this discussion, we have been talking to one another in a dream; and when in a dream, we seem to be narrating dreams, the resemblance of the two states is quite astonishing.'

SOCRATES: 'You see, then, that a doubt about the reality of sense is easily raised, since there may even be a doubt whether we are awake or in a dream. And as our time is equally divided between sleeping and waking, in either sphere of existence the soul contends that the thoughts which are present to our mind at the time are true; and during one half of our lives we affirm the truth of the one, and, during the other half, of the other, and are equally confident of both.'

THEAETETUS: 'Most true.'

SOCRATES: 'And may not the same be said of madness and the other disorders? The difference is only the times are not equal.'[44]

It is obvious that Carroll was interested in this theme, as both of the *Alice* books are dreams, and in *Sylvie and Bruno* "the narrator shuttles back and forth mysteriously between real and dream worlds."[45] "Either I've been dreaming about Sylvie", he comments, "and this is the reality, or else I've really been with Sylvie, and this is a dream! Is Life itself a dream, I wonder?" The reader is led, through these questions, to the uncertain means for distinguishing between the waking and dream states, thus rendering material existence to be the

---

44 Martin Gardner, ed., *The Annotated Alice* (New York: Clarkson N. Potter, Inc., 1960), 90-91.

45 Ibid., 238.

same as a dream. In the words of the Theaetetus, "the resemblance of the two states is quite astonishing." In a letter to Ruskin's cousin and companion, Mrs Joan Agnew Severn, Carroll advises her that he has sent Ruskin a copy of *Sylvie and Bruno* and makes the following comments:

> If he ever cares to know anything about the book, I should like him to be reminded that he expressed a hope, years ago, that my next book would not be a mere unconnected dream... I have tried to do this in *Sylvie and Bruno*—and that the book contains no dreams, this time: what look like dreams are meant for trances—after the fashion of the esoteric Buddhists—in which the spirit of the entranced person passes away into an ACTUAL Fairyland. Believe me.[46]

Many literary critics of the *Sylvie and Bruno* books contend that Carroll used the dream motif as a literary device. There is reason to believe, however, that rather than employing a simple literary device, Carroll was introducing the problem of perception.

If it can be agreed that there is evidence to suggest the possibility of Carroll as a Platonist, with subsequent leanings toward theosophy, then it would follow that there is the possibility that Carroll was obscuring ideology in allegory. Both the *Fama* and *Confessio Fraternitatis* had been addressed to the erudite of Europe and, since the early seventeenth century, many European intellectuals had become familiar with a system of theosophy that revealed meanings obscured in ancient allegorical texts. These men, having abandoned the search for a scientific system that would disclose the truth of Divine nature, found satisfaction in theosophy. Many of Carroll's activities, associations and diary annotations suggest that he, too, leaned in this direction. However, as the prodigy of a conservative Victorian family, it

46 Cohen and Green, *Letters*, vol. 2, 776.

can be assumed that there was incentive for him to be discreet about his less traditional views. Carroll's father, as well as his influential friend Dr Pusey, was a staunch supporter of the old order of Anglican ritual and dogma. Both the elder Dodgson and Dr Pusey had been instrumental in Carroll's formative religious training. However, Carroll, by his own admission, did not share the entirety of their views. Neither did he, however, find satisfaction in the antithetical position of, for example, Huxley or Darwin. It is interesting to note that Huxley, in 1860, coined the term "agnostic" to describe his position. The Latin prefix "a", of course, is employed as a negation to an attached word. Thus, we have Huxley negating the gnosis, or the knowledge of God. Huxley is not necessarily denying the possible existence of God. He is denying, instead, the ability to have knowledge of God. When thus clarified, it can be seen that there are actually some similarities between the agnostic and High Church position. It is extremely unlikely that either of these groups would have conceded that this was the case, but just as agnosticism denied any knowledge of God, neither was such knowledge invited by ritualism. The ritual and rigid dogmatic parameters of the High Church, with its accompanying doctrinal disputes, served as a barrier to, rather than facilitator of, any actual knowledge of Divine Nature. It is quite likely that this is the reason that Carroll failed to find compatibility with either the High Church or agnostic positions. His response, instead, appears to have gravitated toward the available nineteenth century Platonism and its prevalent theosophical, gnostic, accompaniments.

The mystical currents within nineteenth century Christianity were opposed to the notion that ritualism was the custodian of the knowledge of God. These currents maintained that every individual, regardless of creed, had access to the knowledge of God. Where ritualism demanded slavish obedience to creeds and dogma, theosophy pointed the way to knowledge through direct experience. An essential tenet of this position was that nothing sound in the way of philosophy or religion could be built on the foundation of a material being's ordinary sense experience. As long as man accepted the faulty evidence of his physical senses, he was at the mercy of the fashioners of creeds.[47] Likewise, reliance upon the evidence supplied by sense experience rendered man dependent upon the capricious claims of science. Interest in Hellenistic theosophy and gnosticism ran high in England during this period, as evidenced by the London based Theosophical Publishing Society. Although many academicians were involved in these pursuits, discretion was exercised in order to avoid scholarly prejudice. The de-mythologized Carroll, as myth-maker, was able to showcase progressive intellectualism and far-sighted spirituality without being buffeted by the materialism or rationalism of the men by whom he was environed. In theosophical terminology, he became a "mystic citizen of the eternal kingdom."[48]

The myth was as essential to Lewis Carroll as it was to Plato. In appealing to the dream-world consciousness of their readers by brilliant literary representations of its natural products, both of these myth-makers appealed to an experience that was more solid than one might infer from the mere content of the mythology in which they found expression. Plato appealed to that major part of man's nature that was neither articulate nor logical, but felt, and willed and acted.[49] Carroll appealed to man's imagination and sense of wonder, requiring his readers to see the world through the fresh,

---

47 Paul Foster Case, *The True and Invisible Rosicrucian Order* (York Beach, Maine: Samuel Weiser, Inc., 1985), 147.

48 Arthur Edward Waite, *The Real History of the Rosicrucians* (London: William Rider and Son, 1887), 64.

49 J. A. Stewart, *The Myths of Plato* (Hertford, England: Stephen Austin and Sons Ltd., 1905), 44.

unconditioned eyes of a child. The subjective relationship is so intimate between myths and their makers that it is impossible for a reader to remain isolated in a self-constructed conceptual world. Both Platonic and Carrollian mythology go down to the bedrock of human nature, where man is more at one with Universal Nature—more in her secret, than he is at the level of his cognitive faculties.

CHAPTER II

The Maker
behind the Myths

For I think it is Love,
For I feel it is Love,
For I'm sure it is nothing but Love!
Sylvie and Bruno

lexander L. Taylor, in digging beneath the superficial generalities in an attempt to find the essential Carroll, shares "that although it may seem a pity to destroy the Carroll legend, the beautiful story of the brilliant mathematician who revealed his heart only to little children... the man is more interesting than the myth, the truth, or what I have seen of it, better than the fairy-tale."[50] The truth, in fact, may be that Charles Lutwidge Dodgson's philosophical inquiries into the possibility of an immaterial reality that lie beyond the

---

50 Alexander L. Taylor, *The White Knight: A Study of C.L.Dodgson (Lewis Carroll)* (Philadelphia: Dufour Editions, 1963), v.

phenomenal world of time and space, gave rise to Lewis Carroll. Carroll confided to Miss Edith Rix that his "conclusion was to give up the literal meaning of the material body altogether and... accept the idea of the material body as only the 'dress' of the spiritual..."[51] Concurring with this profile of Carroll's philosophy, Alexander L. Taylor, in *The White Knight,* states: "It was a greatly changed Dodgson who emerged from the writing and publication of *Through the Looking-Glass.* In that work he had made it clear to himself; if to nobody else, that his God was a God of Love and a God of Mystery, the world vastly stranger than the churchmen or the scientists realized, the great controversies infinitely petty and ridiculous. He was not understood, nor had he meant to be."[52]

Entertaining the imaginative literature of Lewis Carroll as the resolution of a philosophical struggle, gives substance to the maker behind the myths. The confusion at Oxford, divided by two distinctively different approaches to human existence—both characteristic of the Western mind—positions Carroll's dilemma in a clearer light. Carroll was confronted with the outcroppings of the Enlightenment, which stressed rationality, empirical science, and sceptical secularism; as well as of Romanticism, which perceived the world as a unitary organism. These two worldviews had notable differences in their attitudes toward the phenomena of human awareness. Whereas the scientific examination of the mind "was empirical and epistemological, gradually becoming focused on sense perception, cognitive development and quantitative behavioural studies,"[53] the Romantics' "interest

---

51 Stuart Dodgson Collingwood, *Life and Letters of Lewis Carroll* (New York: The Century Co., 1898), 241.

52 Taylor, *White Knight*, 148.

53 Richard Tarnas, *The Passion of the Western Mind* (New York: Ballantine Books, 1991), 368.

in human consciousness was fuelled by a newly intense sense of self-awareness and a focus on the complex nature of the human self, and was comparatively unconstrained by the limits of the scientific perspective."[54]

Romanticism yearned to explore the mysteries of interiority, of moods and motives, inner conflicts and contradictions, memories and dreams, to bring the unconscious into consciousness, to experience extreme and ineffable states of consciousness, and to know the infinite. "In contrast to the scientist's quest for general laws defining a single objective reality, the Romantic gloried in the unbounded multiplicity of realities pressing in on his subjective awareness, and in the complex uniqueness of each object, event, and experience presented to his soul."[55] The search for a unifying order and meaning was critical for the Romantics, but for genuine cognition, they deemed it necessary to employ a larger range of human faculties. Imagination and subjectivity joined sense and reason to render a deeper understanding of the world. "God was rediscovered in Romanticism—not the God of orthodoxy or deism but of mysticism, pantheism, and immanent cosmic process; not the juridical monotheistic patriarchy but a divinity more ineffably mysterious, pluralistic, all-embracing, neutral or even feminine in gender; not an absentee creator but a numinous creative force within nature and within the human spirit."[56] Carroll's life and literature extolled the imperatives of the Romantic tradition, revealing him as a mystic for whom *Alice* was a Muse.

As Lewis Carroll began to take on a life of his own, the two identities were very clearly, and intentionally, mutually exclusive. "He, ... even in official life, became more and more like two men, Lewis Carroll and Charles Dodgson, sometimes

54 Ibid.
55 Ibid.
56 Ibid., 373.

with an imperative need to keep them apart."[57] When Mrs Bennie, wife of the Rector of Glenfield, asked him if he were the author of *Alice's Adventures,* he exclaimed emphatically, "My dear Madam, my name is Dodgson and *Alice's Adventures* was written by Lewis Carroll."[58] Likewise, when the secretary of a Young Ladies Academy in the United States asked him, in a letter addressed via Christ Church, to present some of his works to the school library, he replied by stating that "Mr Dodgson's books are all on mathematical subjects" and would not be appropriate in a school library.[59] As Edward Guiliano has pointed out, "it was neither accident nor neuroticism that there was no human being corresponding to Lewis Carroll."[60] Lewis Carroll was interested in investigating the possibilities of immaterial realities beyond the phenomenal world and of a truth that transcended ordinary perception.

Dodgson was writing for *The Train,* a literary magazine edited by Edmund Yates, when he selected the name for his immaterial self. Dodgson considered four names as follows: (1) Edgar Cuthwellis, (2) Edgar U. C. Westhall, (3) Louis Carroll and (4) Lewis Carroll. The first two were formed from the letters of his two Christian names, Charles Lutwidge, and the last two were merely variant forms of those names. Editor Edmund Yates guided him in selecting "Lewis" (= Ludovicus = Lutwidge) and "Carroll" (= Carolus = Charles).[61]

Both identities, Charles Lutwidge Dodgson and Lewis Carroll, were prolific. Charles Lutwidge Dodgson contributed

---

57 Phyllis Greenacre, *Swift and Carroll: A Psychoanalytic Study in Two Lives* (New York: International University Press, 1955), 256.

58 Collingwood, *Life and Letters,* 99.

59 Ibid., 273.

60 Edward Guiliano, ed. *Lewis Carroll Observed: A Collection of Unpublished Photographs, Drawings, Poetry and New Essays* (New York: Clarkson N. Potter, Inc., 1976), 79.

61 Collingwood, *Life and Letters,* 67.

a significant amount of published work, in both mathematical and literary circles, during the years 1860–1893. Dodgson wrote an important series of mathematical treatises under his own name, or the initials C.L.D., including *A Syllabus of Plane Algebraic Geometry; The Formula of Plane Trigonometry; Condensation of Determinants; An Elementary Treatise on Determinants; Formulae in Algebra for Responsions; Euclid, Book V, Proved Algebraically; Euclid and His Modern Rivals; Euclid, Books I and II; Curiosa Mathematica, Part I: A New Theory of Parallels; Examples in Arithmetic* and *Symbolic Logic, Part I.*[62]

Another avenue for Dodgson's literary outpouring was what is referred to as his Oxford Squibs and Pamphlets. This group is characterized by socio-political overtones and, though they were all published anonymously, their authorship was an open secret. Among the Oxford Pamphlets are *American Telegrams; The New Method of Evaluation as Applied to Pi; The Dynamics of a Parti-cle; The Elections to the Hebdomadal Council; The Deserted Parks; The Offer of the Clarendon Trustees; The New Belfry at Christ Church, Oxford; The Vision of the Three T's: a Threnody by the Author of 'The New Belfry'; The Blank Cheque, A Fable; Objections, submitted to the Governing Body of Christ Church, Oxford, against certain proposed alterations in the Great Quadrangle; Suggestions as to the Best Method of Taking Votes; Where More Than Two Issues are to be Voted On; Some Popular Fallacies about Vivisection; Professorship of Comparative Philology; Fame's Penny Trumpet; Memoria Technica; Word Links; The Profits of Authorship; Lawn Tennis Tournaments; Parliamentary Elections; Twelve Months in a Curatorship; Curiosissma Curatoria; Circular Billiards; Eight or Nine Wise Words about Letter Writing; Syzygies and*

---

62 For annotations on these works, see Appendix I.

Lanrick and *Pillow Problems, Thought Out During Sleepless Nights.*[63]

The works, though, written as Lewis Carroll were to become the most influential. These consisted of *Alice's Adventures in Wonderland; Through the Looking-Glass and What Alice Found There; Phantasmagoria and Other Poems; The Hunting of the Snark; Rhyme? and Reason?; A Tangled Tale; Sylvie and Bruno (in two parts);* and *Three Sunsets and Other Poems.*[64]

There is an old axiom that one is known by the company that one keeps. Dodgson's circle of close friends, in fact, also sheds some light on the persona of Lewis Carroll. In 1857, Dodgson was introduced to Tennyson through an invitation to photograph the Tennyson family at a private sitting in their home. Dodgson had attained a reputation for being an outstanding portrait photographer and his collection contained photographs of some of the most prestigious men and women of his era. Dodgson was fond of Tennyson's writing and was interested in seeing some original manuscripts that were passing from hand to hand among a select coterie of Tennyson's admirers. However, Dodgson's punctilious code of conduct mandated that he have Tennyson's permission for him to read such manuscripts. These requests angered Tennyson to the degree that he always denied them. Despite Tennyson's contentious nature, Dodgson was able to establish a friendship with the poet, until Dodgson made a serious *faux pas* in the relationship. "The Laureate had been greatly vexed by the pirating of his early poems, a copy of which had come into Dodgson's possession. When Dodgson heard from the bookseller asking him to return it in view of the poet's objections, he wrote to Tennyson begging him to be allowed to keep the book. Any such request was bound to fail with anyone

---

63 For annotations on these works, see Appendix I.
64 For annotations on these works, see Appendix I.

as touchy and irritable as Tennyson, especially as he quite naturally regarded this as a matter of principle."[65]

Tennyson, like Dodgson, had been the son of an English Church clergyman. Currents of thought in nineteenth century England had seriously challenged Tennyson's faith and, although he entertained doubts, he never fully abandoned his Anglican beliefs. George Macdonald, likewise, joined Tennyson and Dodgson in the quest for personal religious clarity. Coming from the plain Calvinism of the Congregational Church in Aberdeenshire, MacDonald freed himself from that harsh and gloomy doctrine of God and, without sacrificing his faith, arrived at a more tolerant and open-minded position. MacDonald was instrumental in convincing Carroll to publish *Alice's Adventures in Wonderland,* because he felt that *Alice* contained a parody of his own *Phantastes* and *Lilith.* There is speculation that Carroll's humorous criticism highlights many crucial aspects of MacDonald's religious exposition, plot structure and literary allusion.[66] One of Dodgson's most dramatic photographs is of George MacDonald, in which he captured the regal air of the writer.

Dodgson's photographs attained an unusually high degree of quality because his approach was that of an artist imbued with a lifetime quest for beauty and perfection. He took his work seriously and often signed his prints "from the artist."[67] Dodgson's interest in the visual arts was not confined, though,

---

65 Anne Clark Amor, *Lewis Carroll: A Biography* (London: Dent Publishing, 1979), 110.

66 Charlie Lovett, review of "The Literary Products of the Lewis Carroll-MacDonald Friendship", by John Docherty, *Knight Letter 48* (Autumn 1994), 3.

67 Edward Guiliano, *Soaring with the Dodo: Essays on Lewis Carroll's Life and Art* (Richmond, Virginia: The Lewis Carroll Society of North America, 1982), 4.

to photography. He was keenly interested in drawing and sketching, and worked diligently to improve his hand skills. He made the acquaintance of John Ruskin in October, 1856, who "in after years was always willing to assist him with his valuable advice on any point of artistic criticism."[68] Dodgson valued the friendship with Ruskin, as evidenced by a letter written to Gertrude Thompson, "Do you know Mr Ruskin? I have the pleasure of numbering him among my friends."[69] He wrote, in another letter to Gertrude Thomson, "I *love* the effort to draw but I utterly fail to please even my own eye— though now and then I seem to get somewhere *near* a right line or two, when I have a live child to draw from.[70] Pre-Raphaelite themes, having sprouted from Romantic poetry and prose, were popular during this period. Dodgson's interest in this genre is supported by his friendships with Dante Gabriel Rossetti, Arthur Hughs, Holman Hunt, Millais, Murro and Watts.[71] Working in this tradition, Dodgson's favourite subjects were nude little girls, representations of Pre-Raphaelite cherubim.

Another passion of Dodgson's was theatre. His love of theatre was so great, in fact, that he prepared a version of *Alice* for the stage. Not all of Dodgson's friends, however, shared this view. Liddon, for example, had been a friend of

---

68 Collingwood, *Life and Letters*, 72.

69 Morton N. Cohen and Roger Lancelyn Green, eds., *The Letters of Lewis Carroll*, vol. 1 (New York: Oxford University Press, 1979), 326.

70 Collingwood, *Life and Letters*, 192.

71 Dante Gabriel Rossetti formed the Pre-Raphaelite Brotherhood in 1848 with William Holman Hunt and Sir John Everett Millais. In 1849, Dante Gabriel Rossetti completed the painting "Childhood of Mary Virgin." In 1884, William Holman Hunt completed the painting "The Triumph of the Innocents". In 1854, Sir John Everett Millais married Effie Gray, who had formerly been the wife of John Ruskin. The Pre-Raphaelite Brotherhood reacted against Victorian materialism and was inspired by medieval and early Renaissance painters up to and including the Italian painter Raphael.

Dodgson's for many years. They had, in fact, toured Russia together in 1867, a journey chronicled in Dodgson's *Russian Journal.* They ultimately parted company, however, as a result of their divergent attitudes about theatre. Whereas Dodgson held it to be a wonderful art-form, Liddon was certain that it led to sin.

Other friends of Dodgson's included the controversial theologian, Edwin Hatch,[72] and John Alexander Stewart, who was White Professor of Moral Philosophy at Oxford, distinguished editor of Aristotle and author of works on Plato. Dodgson counted among his friends John Earle, eminent philologist, essayist and Dante expert; as well as with the distinguished Dante scholar, Edward Moore. Dodgson shared theosophical interests with Max Müller, the eminent nineteenth century German philologist who became the Taylorian Professor of Modern Languages and the first Professor of Comparative Philology at Oxford.

No discussion of Dodgson's friendships, however, would be complete without mentioning his many children friends. The list of female children that he befriended is too long to cite. He was said, in fact, to have initiated new child friendships in trains and other public places with children that he had not previously known. Some of the friendships ended abruptly when the young girls attained adolescence and peer associations replaced the attention of a doting old gentleman. However, several of the relationships endured as the girls metamorphosed into women. Some of the more notable long-term friendships were with Ellen Terry, Edith Rix, Beatrice Earle, Alice Theodora Raikes, Kathleen Savile Clark and, of course, Alice Pleasance Liddell. An accurate account of

---

72 Edwin Hatch (1835-1889) was an English theologian who was best known as the author of the paper *Influence of Greek Ideas and Usages Upon the Christian Church,* which he presented during the 1888 Hibbert Lectures.

Dodgson's friendship with Alice Pleasance Liddell is difficult to extrapolate from the romanticized speculations.

On June 2, 1853, Thomas Gaisford, Dean of Christ Church, suddenly died. He was seventy-six, had been in perfect health, and only one week before his death had been with Dodgson and Osbourne Gordon in the Library, putting away newly acquired books and apparently in perfect health."[73] Pusey maintained that it had been the changes in the old order at the University that had broken Gaisford. He wrote to Gladstone, "this will, at the best, make a very sad change. He was a representative of the best of the past, which has been passing away, and respect for him was a check to revolution in many institutions."[74] Gaisford had, in fact, been very vocal and demonstrative about his dislike of change in the University. Understandably, the appointment of a successor was potentially volatile. Eighteen months earlier, Liddell had preached a very controversial sermon at Oxford subjecting Biblical allegory to the test of reason. In so doing, he had identified himself with Essayists such as Baden-Powell, Pattison and Jowett. Pusey, as an extreme conservative, condemned his sermon, saying, "we must bear the struggle with rationalism: but it is miserable to hear it coming down upon the young men from those who ought to teach them the truth."[75] Dodgson, however, having no personal knowledge of Liddell, reserved his judgement, but made a diary entry noting the general lack of enthusiasm at Christ Church for Liddell's appointment. Alice was the new Dean's daughter.

Dodgson became friendly with Alice, as well as with the other Liddell children. *Alice's Adventures in Wonderland* allegedly had its inception on a mid-summer afternoon's boat-trip that he took with the three girls. Dodgson, however, was

---

73 Clark Amor, *Biography*, 81.
74 Ibid.
75 Ibid., 82.

not an individual who engaged in spontaneity, superficiality or idle recreation. He exercised extreme control over his life and activities, and was compulsively concerned about the productive use of time. Any leisure activity resulted in a necessary didactic by-product. There was absolutely no aspect of Dodgson's life that was not fastidiously attended to and undertaken with utmost meticulousness. The premise that the *Alice* books, therefore, were spontaneously spun on a lazy summer afternoon as casual children's amusement is not consistent with Dodgson's personality profile. Dodgson was a man for whom every move, in literally every area of his life, had exacting intent and purpose and it is, thus, most probably the case that his writing of the *Alice* books was no exception. It is more likely that Dodgson feared the social consequences of exposing his views in plain utterance and, thus, veiled his content in an allegorical system similar to that of the Neoplatonic tradition. With only a cursory reading of the *Alice* and *Sylvie and Bruno* books, it is obvious and public that codes Carroll worked into the text can be found. For example, the poem at the beginning of *Sylvie and Bruno* is an acrostic of his friend Isa Bowman's name. Similarly, the verse at the close of *Through the Looking-Glass* is an acrostic for Alice Pleasance Liddell. Another example is the mathematical puzzle where he questioned the multiplication table's veracity through Alice's distressed concern that she would "never get to twenty at that rate!" Mathematicians can recognize this as a problem based on scales of notation, but even non-mathematicians should make an effort to follow the explanation proposed by Alexander Taylor as it provides evidence that Carroll was doing something quite different from creating an apparently guileless story for children.[76]

---

76 Alexander Taylor, in *The White Knight* (Philadelphia: Dufour Editions, 1963), pp. 46-47, constructs a good explanation of the

Dodgson became a frequent guest in the Liddell home despite his opposition to Liddell's fiscal administration of the college. At some point, however, Mrs Liddell estranged herself from Dodgson, which placed a strain on his relationship with the children. Mrs Liddell's antagonism toward Dodgson marked the beginning of a social distance between he and Alice. On October 17, 1859, the Prince of Wales, Leopold George Duncan Albert, came into residence at Christ Church. Some accounts report that the Prince developed a romantic attraction for Alice and attempted to court her. This relationship, however, did not come to maturity and Alice eventually married Mr Reginald Hargreaves.

One of the strains in Dodgson's relationship with Dean and Mrs Liddell was his outspokenness about University policy. An example of this is seen in Dodgson's challenge to Benjamin Jowett's proposed salary increase. On November 20, 1861, Dodgson addressed a meeting that had met to consider the Dean's proposal to increase the stipend of Benjamin Jowett. Dodgson, a fiscal conservative, was opposed to increasing Jowett's pay. Dodgson argued his position fairly, albeit passionately. In some respects, Dodgson resembled the stoic philosophers, for no outward circumstances could upset the tranquility of his mind. He lived the life that Marcus Aurelius commended so highly, the life of calm contentment, based on the assurance that so long as we are faithful to ourselves, no seeming evils can really harm us. In him, however, was one exception to this rule. During an argument, he was often excited. "The war of words, the keen and subtle conflict between trained minds—in this his soul took delight, in this he sought and found the joy of battle and of victory."[77] However, he would not let his serenity be ruffled by any foe he

mathematical problem of scales of notation as used by Carroll in this setting.

77 Collingwood, *Life and Letters*, 271.

considered unworthy of his steel and he refused to argue with people that were hopelessly illogical.

In October 1881, Dodgson resigned his Mathematical Lectureship in order to "do some worthy work in writing— partly in the cause of mathematical education, partly in the cause of innocent recreation for children, and partly, I hope (though I am utterly unworthy of being allowed to take up such a work) in the cause of religious thought."[78] After this retirement, Dodgson spent a great deal of time with Theo Heaphy, daughter of his old friend Thomas Heaphy, with whom he shared an interest in religion and psychic research.[79]

By 1875, Dodgson was beginning to retreat into a private world in which he effectively barricaded himself against the outside world except a few very close friends and relatives. Around 1887 Dodgson began to be subject to "optical delusions," which took the form of seeing moving apparitions. Many critics attributed this to the strain of incessant work as, during this period of time, he was spending twelve hours a day in reading and writing. Despite his unceasing labors, he died without finishing all of his proposed literary projects. The book on *Great Religious Difficulties* was never completed, although one chapter of it, written in 1895 and circulated privately to family and friends, was published after his death by his nephew, Stuart Dodgson Collingwood, in *The Lewis Carroll Picturebook*. Entitled *Eternal Punishment*, it dealt with the problem of whether the concept of eternal punishment meted out by God was compatible with the belief in the infinite goodness and boundless mercy of God. This theme had been introduced in 1878, by Dr Frederick William Farrar, Dean of Canterbury, in his book *Eternal Hope*.[80] All

---

78 Clark Amor, *Biography*, 218.
79 Ibid.
80 Ibid., 266.

indicators point to Dodgson contending that religion was the revelation of love, rather than a prescribed list of ritual. His outright rejection of the doctrine of eternal damnation was consistent with the refusal to accept any scholastic doctrine that contradicted the love of God. In a letter to an unidentified recipient he openly stated that he had "always felt repelled by the... higher development called 'Ritualism'."[81] Differentiating between a revelation of love and mere ritualism, he continued, "more and more, as I read of the Christian religion, as Christ preached it, I stand amazed at the forms men have given to it, and the fictitious barriers they have built up between themselves and their brethren."[82] Dodgson proclaimed having "the knowledge of Jesus Christ," but this knowledge was not confined to a ritualistic Anglicanism. It appeared more gnostic in substance, having a direct bearing on the welfare of the individual human being and on the development of a more harmonious social order. This religious philosophy, being more theosophical in nature, provided a system of discerning the fundamental truths of Divine nature through ancient allegorical texts. Among notable students of this esoteric tradition were John Picus de Mirandola and Elias Ashmole, both of whose philosophical works were familiar to Dodgson.

In the early seventeenth century many European academicians were familiar with a system of theosophy that provided keys to the inner meanings of Neoplatonic, Hermetic and Gnostic allegories. This system was expressed in cryptic language and for the following two centuries exerted considerable influence on European thought. When *Fama Fraternitatis* was issued as a manuscript and circulated among German theosophists in 1610, it reflected that

---

81 Cohen and Green, *Letters*, vol. 1, 463.
82 Ibid.

influence. Elias Ashmole,[83] in fact, incorporated the substance of a whole paragraph from the *Fama* in the introduction of *Theatrum Chemicum Britannicum*, a collection of alchemical texts by English adepts.[84] Thus, we trace what adherents would call an "invisible chain of transmission" of Platonic, Neoplatonic, Hermetic and Gnostic doctrines. This ancient gnosis may be viewed as a knowledge of the nature of man and of his place in the universe which transcends the appearance of things as presented to the senses, as well as knowledge derived from reason, which contacts reality in a region of pure Truth. Since the beginning of this knowledge is the realization that things are not as they seem, materialism does not provide an adequate approach to this knowledge. Max Müller[85] wrote in *Theosophy of Psychological Religion* that although many of the early Church Fathers had been instructed in gnosis, their teachings gradually became limited to the more restrictive and materialistic dogmas and creeds.[86] Dodgson's diaries and letters document his friendship with Müller and suggest that he shared this sentiment. Victorian Christianity had misled

---

83 Elias Ashmole (1617–1692) was a late, but ardent, student of John Dee, whose manuscripts he possessed, and an apologist for Rosicrucianism. Some historians believe that Ashmole was the actual founder of Speculative Freemasonry, basing the fraternity on ideas from Francis Bacon's *New Atlantis*.

84 Paul Foster Case, *The True and Invisible Rosicrucian Order* (York Beach, Maine: Samuel Weiser, Inc., 1985), 36.

85 Max Müller (1823–1900) was a German born British Philologist and Orientalist, one of the founders of Indian studies, who virtually created the discipline of comparative religion. Müller wrote both scholarly and popular works on this subject, a discipline he introduced to the British reading public. The *Sacred Books of the East*, a massive, 50-volume set of English translations prepared under his direction, stands as an enduring monument to Victorian scholarship.

86 William Kingsley, *The Gnosis or Ancient Wisdom in the Christian Scriptures* (London: George Allen and Unwin Ltd., 1937), 84.

people into thinking that truth was attained through belief in certain dogmas and Dodgson simply outgrew the rigid confines of the conservative Anglican system. Commensurately, neither was he comfortable with the liberal counter-position that faith must *necessarily* conform to the limits of reason.

The fairy duet sung by Sylvie and Bruno provides a key to understanding Carroll's position. In this duet, Carroll's vision of Love is presented as the embodiment of the Spirit of God and symbolizes an essential knowledge of Ultimate Reality.

> 'Tis a secret, and so let us whisper it low—
> And the name of the secret is Love!

This is the quintessence of Carroll's spirituality, identifying Love as the sole principle in religious experience. Indicative of the nineteenth century theosophical intellectual hymn to Love, it is unique in its theological sophistication and esoteric qualities.[87] The fundamental premise was that "of God's nature in Itself we can and do know one thing only—that it is transcendent Love."[88] This is one of the most distinctive features of true mysticism, setting it apart from every other kind of transcendental theory and practice. "It is the eager, outgoing activity whose driving power is generous love, not the absorbent, indrawing activity which strives only for new knowledge, that is fruitful in the spiritual as well as in the physical world."[89] In this sense, love is to be understood as the ultimate expression of the self's most vital tendencies, and

---

87 C. G. Harrison, *The Transcendental Universe*. Introduction by Christopher Bamford. (Hudson, New York: Lindisfarne Press, 1993), 14.
88 Ibid., 15.
89 Evelyn Underhill, *Mysticism* (New York: E. P. Dutton & Co., Inc., 1911), 85.

not as a superficial affection or emotion. "Mystic Love is a total dedication of the will; the deep-seated desire and tendency of the soul towards its Source. It is a condition of humble access, a life-movement of the self: more direct in its methods, more valid in its results—even in the hands of the least lettered of its adepts—than the most piercing intellectual vision of the greatest philosophical mind."[90] It is impossible to limit mystical truth to the doctrine of any one religious system. The mystic only feels thoroughly natural, fully alive, when he is obeying the voice of Love. For him, Love, as opposed to ritual, provides the source of joy, the secret of the universe and the vivifying principle of all things.

The first volume of *Sylvie and Bruno* contains strong criticism of ritualism, charging that it involved the danger of regarding church services as an end in themselves rather than as a means to produce fruit in human lives and society. In a letter to Miss Ellen Terry, Carroll stated that he was "going to be very bold, and make a suggestion... that the clause in the sentence of Shylock, 'That, for this favour, he presently became a Christian,' be omitted. It is a sentiment that is entirely horrible and revolting to the feelings of all who believe in the Gospel of Love. To all Christians now (except perhaps extreme Calvinists) the idea of forcing a man to adjure his religion, whatever that religion may be, is... simply horrible."[91]

The *Sylvie and Bruno* books are a mystic's primers on the deep-seated desire and tendency of the soul towards its Source. Carroll's hero, Arthur, practically recites Plotinus[92] as he instructs Lady Muriel that one's goal should be to aspire

90 Ibid.
91 Ibid., 183.
92 Plotinus is considered to be the founder of Neoplatonism. Inspired by his reading of Plato, Plotinus developed a complex spiritual cosmology involving three hypostases: the One, the Intelligence, and

"to the highest motive of all, the desire for likeness to, and union with, the Supreme Good." Plotinus' first Divine Hypostasis is the prime source and principle of all being whatsoever and is called the One or the Good. Poetically, Plotinus likens it to a stream that is its own source.[93] The second Divine Hypostasis is the sphere of absolute reality, the Universal Intelligence; and the third Divine Hypostasis is the Universal Soul, which is the image of the second Divine Hypostasis. Universal Soul differs from Universal Intelligence in that its life is not perfectly impassive. Universal Soul perpetually revolves about and within the sphere of Intelligence, aspiring to and attaining the Supreme Good through *the medium of the Beautiful*.[94] To be certain that this point wasn't missed, Carroll deemed Prince Uggug, who was *ugly in both appearance and nature*, "Loveless, loveless!" and, as punishment, had him turned into a porcupine and confined to a barren cage. Summarizing Prince Uggug's fate, and driving Carroll's point home, the Emperor instructs Sylvie and Bruno, "See the fate of a loveless life?"

Universal Soul is generally sufficiently evolved within us that we can be said to possess it. Universal Intelligence, on the other hand, may be regarded as overshadowing us, and it is only in exceptional individuals and under favourable circumstances that its effulgence irradiates one's mind. As regards the supreme principle of the One or the Good, its presence in our soul is mere potentiality.

Plotinus defines Love as the desire to be united with a beautiful object, and thereby produce or create beauty. Love is always the result of an affinity, conscious or otherwise, between the soul of the lover and the object of his or her

---

the Soul. It is from the productive unity of these three Beings that all existence emanates.

93 Plotinus, *The Enneads*, Ennead III, sec. 9.
94 Plotinus, *The Enneads*, Ennead IV, sec. 16.

passion. Our desire to produce is the direct outcome of the soul's instinctive craving for immortality, since the essence of immortality is none other than Beauty itself.

The vital harmony and unity of the material universe is an image of the essential unity of the universal being. Potentially, matter is the infinite sum of derivative being, but in actuality it is absolute nonentity—the infinite, the indefinite, the formless—abstractly conceivable only by virtue of a mental process that implies the suspension of true intellection. Matter is capable of receiving a semblance of determinate existence by reflecting the forms derived by the Universal Soul from the Intelligible Universe, but in itself it remains unchanged and unchangeable. Plotinus likens it to a mirror in which we behold not objects themselves but merely the images or reflections of objects. Plotinus' mirror became Carroll's looking glass. Though omnipresent, it is invisible, and naturally leads us to attribute reality to the illusive images we behold in it. These are, however, merely fleeting phenomena of the sensible universe and hold an intermediate position between reality and negation. This is seen in *Sylvie and Bruno's* Outland where every part, even the remote, is allied by an intimate bond of vital sympathy.

The existence of the Universal Soul is essentially an active and eternal contemplation of the Good as revealed in the sphere of Intelligence. Thus, the Universal Soul is an indivisible, non-corporeal essence whose property is to be present as a whole in each one of its parts or faculties. It is, then, the last essence of the intelligible and the first in the material order. This is Carroll's Borderland, the place between Outland and Fairyland. In Outland, or the material realm, it is impossible to distinguish between reality and illusion. Carroll makes this clear when his Narrator claims, "so, either I've been dreaming about Sylvie, and this is the reality or else I've really been with Sylvie, and this is a dream!" Access to

Fairyland, or Universal Intelligence, on the other hand, is acquired "from within." When Lady Muriel, for example, invited Sylvie to play the piano, "she seated herself at the instrument and began instantly. Time and expression… were perfect; and her touch was one of such extraordinary lightness that it was at first scarcely possible.…" Sylvie's playing had been marvelous, like "the tinkle of the last dew drops, shaken from the trees by a passing gust— such that one saw the first glittering rays of the sun, breaking through the clouds." When the parlour guests begged Sylvie to disclose the name of the opera or air that she had played, she confessed that she did not know what either an opera or an air was! The knowledge of the music had come "from within," and was not the product of training or technique. Sylvie, albeit exceptionally illumined through Universal Intelligence, had however, not yet ascended to Elfland. Herein dwelt the Supreme Good, where all things found perfect union. As Sylvie made her approach to Elfland, her spiritual sight had not yet become sufficient to see things as they were. There was no material essence and, therefore, no separation. She was troubled by the lack of material definition of individual objects, and asked, "Are they *all* like that, father?" Her father replied, "They're all like that to *you*, darling, because you don't belong to Elfland—yet. But to *me* they are real."

The Universal Soul dwells in Borderland. It has two parts, a principal part that inhabits the sphere of Intelligence and an inferior part that proceeds toward the sensible world. Thus, although the essential life of the Universal Soul is a contemplation and desire of a superior principle, its powers are not exhausted by this effort. The Generative Power which proceeds from the essence of the Universal Soul is personified as Nature, and as an image of the Principle Power is, therefore, an inferior principle. Everything in Nature possesses an individual soul that, like the Universal Soul of which it is a member, contemplates the intelligible order. However, by virtue of its lower irrational or strictly natural soul, it is in immediate vital or sympathetic relation with the rest of the material universe. In nineteenth century *philosophia occulta,* an initiate referred to one who was able to penetrate the "region of super-physical concepts" that was "hidden by a thin veil from the world of sense, and to distinguish between illusions and realities, which, *on the Borderland* are in close juxtaposition to each other."[95]

The Universal Soul, regarded as the principle of Nature, is then both one and many. It seeks to reconcile the extremes of integrity and aloofness, of universality and individuality. In the Universal Intelligence, this reconciliation of opposites, which appears in Nature as a perpetual, albeit never accomplished, process, is absolute and eternal. Nature is both unity and multiplicity.

The mind can only be satisfied by that which simultaneously appeals to, and gains approval of, the heart, as well. Then the soul, which formerly experienced no rapture, can renounce its attitude of impartiality, awaken invigorated, and begin its ascent under the sweet influence of Love. Thus liberated, it soars by the aid of reminiscence to a higher principle than the object of its immediate contemplation. This ecstatic reunion with the Good leaves the soul permanently beautified and enlightened and is an act of contemplation of all existence.

For the Neoplatonist, the Good is the ultimate destination to which the soul aspires. It is the source and goal of all living things, the principle of evolution and involution, the expulsive energy and the attractive force. It is the ultimate anthropic principle, the circle that closes on itself. In one word, it is Love. This is the sole principle of ascension. However, souls that have contemplated the Good may return to reveal to others the secret of celestial rapture, which seems to justify

---

95 Harrison, *Transcendental Universe,* 91.

the conclusion that Love is, or at least should be, also the descending principle. The individual soul knows no rest until it has completed its circuit and returned to the Source from whence it was derived. Thus, duality is overcome as the soul achieves unity with the Good. In *Alice in Wonderland,* although the stage is set, there are still traces of duality. By *Sylvie and Bruno*, however, all remnants of dualism had given way to unity. The Carroll who penned *Sylvie and Bruno,* by his own admission, had been set free from the shackles of nineteenth century Anglican ritualism. He had come to a rich awareness that human spirituality was not contingent upon dogma or doctrine; and his soul grew wings as he made his own ascent, through incrementally higher degrees of Love.

In 1898, Dodgson, turned Lewis Carroll, had an eight-day battle with influenza which resulted in his death. It could be said that his life was reflected in the old story of *Eyes and No Eyes*. In the story, *No Eyes* has fixed his attention on the fact that he is obliged to take a walk. He intends to accomplish this task as efficiently and comfortably as he can. "He asks not to know what may be on either side of the hedges. He ignores the caress of the wind until it threatens his hat. He trudges along, steadily, diligently; avoiding the muddy pools, but oblivious to the light which they reflect."[96] *Eyes*, too, takes the same walk, but for him it is a perpetual revelation of beauty and wonder. "The sunlight inebriates him, the winds delight him, the very effort of the journey is a joy. Magic presences throng the roadside, or cry salutations to him from the hidden fields. The rich world through which he moves lies in the foreground of his consciousness; and it gives up new secrets to him at every step."[97] Lewis Carroll took the walk of

---

96 Evelyn Underhill, *Practical Mysticism* (New York: E. P. Dutton & Co., Inc., 1915), 10.
97 Ibid.

Eyes, moving not only himself, but anyone who cared to peer through the looking-glass, into the rich world of mystical consciousness.

CHAPTER III

The Minds behind the Mystic

*T*he fundamental distinction between post-Renaissance England's competing worldviews was in what each considered to be the nature of primary reality. The Platonists assumed the primacy of mind and viewed nature as a system of appearances, or images, in which a metaphysical order was reflected. The first beginnings of the opposite view were associated with Aristotle, in whom the naturalistic bias was strong. During the Renaissance, there began to be a shift towards the reliance on quantitative science provided by natural or humanistic philosophy. Spokesmen of that era cited this change as an "advance from ignorance and magic" to "knowledge and material science."[98] Consequently, during this period philosophy became dominated by humanist and

---

98 Kathleen Raine and George Mills Harper, *Thomas Taylor The Platonist: Selected Writings* (Princeton: Princeton University Press, 1969), 5.

empirical premises, which stemmed, in large part, from Locke and Berkeley.

It could be said that empiricism argues the existence of God through knowledge of the material world, whereas the mystic experiences the material world through knowledge of God. Empiricism delights in the multiplicity of the phenomenal web. It is concerned with individual parts as opposed to the whole, and its method is one of particularizing the universal. This approach attempts to quantify the universal, through a reduction of form and qualitative relations to mathematical and statistical formulations based on the perception of material objects. By contrast, mysticism is concerned with the whole as opposed to the part. Realizing that all things are essentially related to certain eternal forms and principles, the mystic experiences the relationship that the particular has with the universal. From this perspective, it is possible to relate the temporal with the eternal and to know the organic relation between multiplicity and unity.[99]

If the mystical spirit is seen as a desire to know the universe in its totality, it might be concluded that both approaches are complementary and necessary in inquiry, for an inclusive cosmology must be equally at home in dealing with the part or the whole. That is to say that one might be most happily at home in the universe by relating one's experiences to both the universal and the particular, the eternal and the temporal levels of being. Hence, the mystic recognizes the wisdom in actively integrating the particular and the universal aspects of being, rather than attempting to build a system of thought exclusively from either "the top down," deduced, for example, from purely *a priori* formulations, or from "the bottom up," abstracting observations only from particular phenomena while ignoring universal principles. This combined method

---

99 Kenneth Sylvan Guthrie, *The Pythagorean Sourcebook and Library* (Grand Rapids, Michigan: Phanes Press, 1987), 44.

could be considered Pythagorean, as the harmonic proportion, for example, exists as a purely universal principle, but would never have been discovered without empirical experimentation on the monochord. Thus, through a creative dialectic between the temporal and the eternal, a form of integration occurs between otherwise purely theoretic and pragmatic methods.[100]

Such a view was, of course, not popularly accepted in nineteenth century academic England. Here the advance of empiricism was creating a climate in which, for example, mathematics would lose its stature as a pure or universal science and would ultimately be transformed into merely a servile nursemaid of applied technology. For one with mystical inclination, there were ideas that could not be understood by ordinary experience that were explained by Plato's theory of reminiscence. This theory furnished a vehicle by means of which one could account for a recurring sensation of having known something in another state or existence. The revival of Platonism during this period, thus, threw open the door to the growing interest in psychical research. The works of the Society for Psychical Research, the Ashmolean Society, and the Dialectical Society culminated in a report (1869) that concluded that psychic phenomena were genuine and pointed to laws and forces that had not been explored by science.[101] If the mind or spirit could live independently of the physical body, then the ground was cut away from the feet of materialism. The materialists were saying that the flame could not exist when the candle was gone, but here were flames a long way from the candle, existing on their own. Carroll plays with this theme in the first chapter of *Alice in Wonderland* when Alice worries about shrinking to the point that she might "go out altogether, like a candle." Then "she tried to fancy

100 Ibid., 47.
101 Arthur Conan Doyle, *The New Revelation* (New York: George H. Doran Co., 1918), 30.

what the flame of a candle looks like after the candle is blown out, for she could not remember ever having seen such a thing." Although Alice's memory was in question, the existence of the phenomena was not. For those interested in this research, the value of determining the existence of psychic phenomena consisted of the fact that it could support and give objective reality to an immense body of knowledge.

As such, mystical trends emerged as a counter-position to the empiricism that was gaining popularity in nineteenth century England. Locke's inquiry, for example, asked how the mind comes to be furnished with its vast store of ideas and the materials of knowledge. His answer was that all knowledge was founded upon, and ultimately derived from, experience. He rejected the premise that some knowledge, such as moral principles or the principle of a whole being equal to all of its parts, was innate. His dismissal was based on the condition that the knowledge that all wholes were equal to the sum of their parts, for example, presupposed the idea of *whole, part,* and *number.* It is these ideas that come from experience. Therefore, what experience provides in these instances is not knowledge itself, but the ideas that form the material basis for knowledge. Locke's real target was not the innateness of ideas, but the innateness of knowledge. His premise was that no knowledge could be innate unless its materials or constituent ideas were.[102]

Locke claimed that, prior to existence, the mind is "white paper, void of all characters" and that all its ideas and the materials of knowledge come from experience. Experience, in fact, provides a dual source of ideas in that some come from our sensory interaction with the world, while others come from our perception of the operation of our own mind as it reflects upon the ideas it has gotten from sensation. Whereas it is

---

102 R. S. Woolhouse, *The Empiricists*, (Oxford: Oxford University Press, 1988), 76.

plausible to assert that our ideas of various colours, material things, or processes and activities derive from experiences, how do we account for the ideas that we have, for example, of a centaur, or of infinity? We have no experience of the objects of these ideas. To cope with this problem, Locke distinguished between *complex* ideas and *simple* ideas. Although simple ideas are directly beholden to experience, complex ideas are constructed of individual parts that have come from experience. Carroll's Mock Turtle, as drawn by Tenniel with the head, hind hooves and tail of a calf affixed to a tortoise's body represents the type of complex idea that Locke would have distinguished as a *substance*. Substances are the *substratum* in which complex ideas subsist, and from which they do result. When the Queen of Hearts asked Alice if she had seen the Mock Turtle, and Alice replied that she "does not know what a Mock Turtle is", one gets a glimpse of Carroll's discomfort with Locke's materialism.

Modes were the second type of complex ideas that Locke identified. Modes do not subsist by themselves, but are considered to be dependent upon substances. In Locke's view, they seemed to represent ways in which the substances on which they depend may be ordered, organized, or arranged. For example, a triangle is not a material thing, but a shape that material things may have or an arrangement into which material things can be put. Locke describes modes as combinations of independent ideas that are put together by the mind. This element of Locke's epistemology would have been less at odds with Carroll's views. Locke's claim that the perception of connections between ideas constituted knowledge allowed geometry, for example, to be viewed as a body of "certain and universal knowledge" obtained by *a priori* intuition or demonstration. Generally, empiricists viewed any purported knowledge obtained by *a priori* perception of connection between ideas as trifling and void of content. In this respect, Locke deviated from a purely empirical position.

Geometrical figures were not the only modes. The ideas of morality were modes, too, and Locke thought that, with proper application, a systematic science of ethics similar to that of mathematics and geometry could be developed. Locke felt that the Bible provided man with a perfect body of ethics that could be arrived at through reason. Locke defined the relation and interplay between knowledge and reason on one hand, and faith, belief and revelation on the other. For Locke, *faith* was a belief that was based on the revelation of the Gospels rather than on experience and observation. He asserted that reason had supremacy over revelation, and that revelation must be answerable to reason. This means that nothing contrary to reason could be accepted on the basis of supposed revelation. This tenet, of course, struck at the very heart of mysticism. It was contrary, as well, to the influential position of the Cambridge Platonists who maintained that if by the term *God* we mean an infinite, spiritual and/or immaterial Being, then reason can tell us nothing at all about Him since terms such as *spiritual* and *immaterial* are not intelligible unless they are used to connote the invisible body.[103] Cudworth, in his *True Intellectual System of the Universe* (1678), defended a spiritualistic interpretation of the Universe as a foundation for the Christian moral life. He reduced materialism to sensationalism and re-affirmed the position of Plato in the *Theaetetus* that sense perception is not knowledge.[104] He continued that it is evident that we have ideas of many things that are not perceptible by the senses. Therefore, we cannot legitimately deny the existence of a being

---

103 Frederick Copleston, *The History of Philosophy,* vol.5, ed. Edmund F. Sutcliffe (Westminster, Maryland: The Newman Press, 1959), 52.
104 Ibid., 56.

simply because it cannot be perceived by the senses. Although Cudworth had been influenced by Descartes, he rejected the latter's sharp dichotomy between the spiritual and material worlds. Henry More, a fellow Cambridge Platonist, demonstrated an even more pronounced hostility toward this Cartesian principle. As a young man, More had been an enthusiastic advocate of Descartes, but his subsequent interest in theosophy caused him to dismiss the Cartesian notion of a material world consisting of extension sharply separated from a spiritual reality.[105]

Cudworth, in his *Treatise Concerning Eternal and Immutable Morality,* stated that there were two kinds of "perceptive cognitions" in the soul. One type was the passive perception of the soul, which could either be sensation, image or phantasm. The second were the active perceptions that arise from the mind itself without the body, and were called "conceptions of the mind." These virtually innate ideas were imprinted on the human mind by God, and by them one knows both immaterial and material objects and truths. Knowledge, as opposed to belief, must be real, stable and unchanging. Thus, the world of sense experience could not satisfy the criteria of knowledge. For example, one may see a certain thing as beautiful, while another sees the same thing as ugly. Carroll's Cheshire-Cat made a point of telling Alice that "a dog growls when it's angry," while he "growls when he's pleased." Alice, in turn, corrected him by clarifying that he did not growl, but purred. The Cat's unassumingly reply, "call it what you like," points up Carroll's view regarding the instability and unreliability of sensory experience.

Berkeley's philosophy added another influential, albeit controversial, voice to the empirical tide washing over nineteenth century England. Starting with the belief in an immaterial God, and perceiving mind or souls, Berkeley then

---

105 Ibid., 60.

went one step further and claimed that this is all there is. All of the "furniture of the earth" does not have any subsistence without a perceiving mind.[106] Berkeley's claims that his particular immaterialism avoided scepticism and restored philosophy to the beliefs of sound common sense were not generally accepted. His view that there was no reality other than minds and their ideas was taken to be scepticism run riot. Saying that he ought to be able to get through a closed door as easily as an open one, Dean Swift is supposed to have left Berkeley standing on the doorstep. Dr Samuel Johnson similarly begged a Berkeleyan not to leave the group he was with "for we may perhaps forget to think of you, and then you will cease to exist."[107] Carroll reflects this sentiment when the March Hare encouraged Alice to "have some wine." Alice, in turn, looked all around the table only to find tea. When she remarked, "I don't *see* any wine," the March Hare was quick to conclude that "then there isn't any." The Berkeleyan theme is suggested again in the discussion of the Red King's dream. And, while the Tweedle brothers defend Bishop Berkeley's position that all material things, including themselves, are only "sorts of things" in the mind of God, Alice takes the common-sense approach of Samuel Johnson with her insistence that she and her tears were, indeed, very real.[108]

Berkeley felt that previous attempts to construct a theory of knowledge erred in supposing a difference between *things* and *ideas*. According to Berkeley, once a distinction is made between perceptions of material things and those things themselves, scepticism results. For it follows from this distinction that only the appearance of things, and not the things themselves, are perceived. This view is fundamentally

---

106 Woolhouse, *Empiricists*, 109.
107 Ibid., 113.
108 Martin Gardner, ed., *The Annotated Alice* (New York: Clarkson N. Potter, Inc., 1960), 238.

incongruent with a Platonic doctrine of the Forms. Although both epistemologies involve immaterialism, the nature of the immaterialism differs significantly. Plato's immaterialism viewed material objects as imperfect reflections or shadows of real, stable and unchanging Forms that existed independently of perception. In Berkeley's system, however, material objects were dependent upon perception by the mind of God. He thus collapses the problem of the distinction between things and ideas by concluding that ideas are things. This is not to say that there are ideas and no things. He does not deny the existence of a world of things. He is denying, instead, a world of objects *beyond direct perception,* which strikes at the very heart of Platonic theory. In the introduction to the *Principles,* Berkeley spends considerable time arguing against the doctrine of abstract ideas. This doctrine's admission of the existence of particular things that we perceive, as well as universals, which are essentially general, was repugnant to Berkeley. For Berkeley, an idea must be an idea of a particular and cannot be abstract. Further, Berkeley contended that the concepts of absolute, as well as relative, time, motion and space wrongly supposed that those qualities could exist without mind.

This contention led Berkeley directly into an attack on mathematicians, saying that they were involved in the "errors arising from the doctrine of abstract ideas, and the existence of objects without the mind."[109] Berkeley continued that mathematicians fail to see that the function of numerical symbols and signs is to provide a means to deal in general ways with groups of particular sensible things. Mathematicians think, instead, that numerical symbols stand for abstract ideas of *number,* which they take to be the province of their subject. This misconception has meant that their work has not been "subservient to practice," and able to "promote

---

109 Woolhouse, *Empiricists,* 129.

the benefit of life." It meant that it has been "abstracted from all use and practice" and has become a purely speculative matter of "high flights and abstractions."[110] In Berkeley's view, since numerals do not stand for "numbers in abstract", but for "particular things numbered," the misguided interest in the properties of such abstractions has really been a trifling concern with mere language or formalism. It was, therefore, a feature of Berkeley's empiricism that pure mathematics was seen as merely the result of formal symbolic manipulation, and not as a substantive body of genuine knowledge.

With regard to geometers, Berkeley contended that their work was misdirected by a false belief in abstract ideas and the mistake that objects of sense exist without the mind. These mistakes have led to the belief that *extension*, the subject matter of geometry, is infinitely divisible. In Berkeley's system, finite extension was not infinitely divisible. Any particular finite extension was simply an idea in our minds, and could not have more parts than the finite number was perceived to have.

It is unlikely that these Berkeleyan themes would have appealed to Carroll. Carroll subscribed to the doctrine of abstraction, both as a mathematician and a geometer. His text, *Examples of Arithmetic* (1876) was a treatise on pure mathematics, with an outline of examples and proofs. Similarly, his devotion to Euclidean principles was whole-hearted. *Euclid, Book V, Proved Algebraically* (1874), *Euclid and His Modern Rivals* (1879), *Euclid, Books I and II* (1882), and *Curiosa Mathematica, Part I: A New Theory of Parallels* (1888) were all attempts to demonstrate the absolute truth of Euclidean theory. Carroll was celebrated in mathematical circles during his lifetime for his renowned defence of Euclid. An April 12, 1879 issue of *Vanity Fair* was quoted as claiming that "Mr Dodgson vivisects all the modern Euclids

110 Ibid., 130.

mercilessly, exposes their fallacies and their vanity with a master-hand, and then cages them in some *reductio ad absurdum* from which there is no escape." It was reported in *English Mechanic and World of Science* (May 2, 1879) that, "Mr Dodgson has shown... that, whatever merits individual works may possess, there has not as yet appeared one destined to supplant Euclid's *Elements of Geometry.*"[111] Historical evidence suggests that Euclid was heavily influenced by Platonic philosophy. It is quite likely that he received his early mathematical education in Athens from the pupils of Plato. Proclus, the fifth century Neoplatonist, asserts that Euclid was of the school of Plato and "intimate with his philosophy." According to Proclus, Euclid "collected many of the theorems of Eudoxus, perfected many of those of Theaetetus, and also brought to incontrovertible demonstration the things which were only loosely proven by his predecessors."[112] Among the extant works of Euclid are the *Data*, for use in the solution of problems by geometric analysis and the *Phenomena*, a treatise on the geometry of the sphere. His lost *Elements of Music* may have provided the basis for the extant *Sectio Canonis* on the Pythagorean theory of music. "Of his lost geometrical works all except one belonged to higher geometry."[113] Thus, history makes room for the assumption that Euclid championed a philosophy that accepted the reality of numbers, figures and their properties independent of human ideas.

Berkeley's contention that infinite divisibility was an error would, further, not be compatible with Carroll's view. In the

---

111 Morton N. Cohen and Roger Lancelyn Green, eds., *The Letters of Lewis Carroll*, vol. 1 (New York: Oxford University Press, 1979), 336.

112 Proclus, *A Commentary on the First Book of Euclid's Elements*, trans. Glenn R. Morrow (Princeton: Princeton University Press, 1992), 426.6.

113 Robert Maynard Hutchins, ed. *Great Books of the Western World*, vol. 11 (Chicago: University of Chicago, 1952), v.

earlier reference to Biddle, Carroll was purported to have said that although infinite divisibility was inconceivable, it was certainly not to be considered impossible, due to the limitations of human reason.[114]

Another tenet of Berkeley's philosophy was his claim that if we allow a distinction between our perceptions of material things and those things themselves, then it follows that we see only the appearances of things, "so that for aught we know, all we see, hear and feel may be only phantom and vain chimera and not at all agree with the real things."[115] Despite Berkeley's claim that he did not make things into ideas, but, instead, ideas into things, the feeling remained that Berkeley had banished all that was real and substantial out of the world and that everything had been made into "so many chimeras and illusion on the fancy."[116] Berkeley proceeded to demonstrate that with only ideas at his disposal, he could nevertheless distinguish between reality and illusion. There was, according to Berkeley, a *rerum natura* that assured that the distinction between realities and chimeras retained its full force even though they both equally existed in the mind and, in that sense, were like *ideas*. He pointed out that sometimes we have control over our ideas and sometimes we do not. He then went on to distinguish between "ideas of sense" and "ideas of imagination". Perceptions of reality were a matter of having "ideas of sense," which had the characteristic of being involuntary and not subject to our control, of being strong and lively, and of having a coherence and order. Illusions, dreams and fancies, on the other hand, consisted of "ideas of imagination" which were voluntary and subject to our wills,

114 Cohen and Green, *Letters,* vol. 1, 589.
115 George Berkeley, *Principles of Human Knowledge and Three Dialogues,* ed. Howard Robinson (New York: Oxford University Press, 1999), 62.
116 Woolhouse, *Empiricists,* 119.

and which lacked both lively strength and orderly coherence.[117] It appeared to have escaped Berkeley's attention, however, that not all imaginary perceptions are voluntary and lacking vivacity. Similarly, he overlooked the fact that when one wills oneself to imagine something, one can make one's ideas as orderly and coherent as one chooses. Thus, Berkeley had not conclusively resolved the troublesome problem of distinguishing between illusion and reality.

According to Berkeley, real things were dependent upon, and did not exist outside of, perceiving minds. According to common sense, however, they were independent of our perception of them. In Berkeley's philosophy, God had the role of accounting for the continued perception of real objects apart from our actual perception of them. However, this explanation failed to solve a further problem. Besides having a continuous existence independent of perception, the real things of common sense were public. Berkeley's account of continuity seemed unable to explain publicity in any way sufficiently akin to that of the perception-independent world of common sense.

For Berkeley, an idea had to be an idea of a particular, and could not be abstract. He spent considerable time arguing against the doctrine of abstract ideas and asserted that any discussion of absolute, as well as relative, time, motion, and space wrongly supposed that those qualities could exist without mind. He continued along these lines by contending that there were no such things as *abstract general ideas,* although he was prepared to admit general ideas in some sense. His view was that "an idea, which considered in itself is particular, becomes general by being made to represent all other particular ideas of the same sort."[118] Thus, universality did not consist "in the absolute positive nature or conception

117 Ibid., 120
118 Copleston, *History of Philosophy,* vol.5, 218.

of anything, but in the relation it bears to the particulars signified or represented by it."[119] If there were no abstract general ideas, it followed that reasoning must be about particulars. Berkeley did not, of course, deny that there were *general words*. However, he rejected Locke's theory that general words denote general ideas, if this were interpreted to mean that ideas possessed a positive universal content. A proper name, such as Humpty Dumpty, signified a particular thing, while a general word signified a plurality of things of a certain kind. Its universality, according to Berkeley, was a matter of use or function. Once this is established, one is spared the task of hunting for elusive entities that correspond to general words. The term "material substance" can be used without it denoting any abstract general idea. Berkeley's nominalism is, therefore, of importance in his attack on Locke's theory of material substance.[120] "Matter" is not a name in the way that "Humpty Dumpty" is a name. Carroll's story about Humpty Dumpty is suggestive of a satirization of Berkeley's nominalism. Humpty Dumpty, from this perspective, subscribed to an extreme form of nominalism, according to which all that is common to a group of particulars is their being called by the same name. When Alice saw Humpty balanced on the top of the wall, she exclaimed, "And how exactly like an egg he is!" To this, Humpty replied that it was "very provoking to be called *an* egg." Alice then assured him that he only resembled the common group of particulars called "eggs" by stating that, "I said you *looked* like an egg, Sir." When Humpty turned the tables on Alice by asking her to tell him her name, she innocently replied, "My *name* is Alice, but—". Humpty retorted that it was a "stupid name enough!" and asked her what it meant. Alice asked Humpty, "Must a name mean something?" and Humpty assured her

119 Ibid., 219.
120 Ibid., 220.

that "of course it must." As if Carroll wanted to be certain that his point was not missed, he had Humpty continue to explain, "My name means the shape I am.... With a name like yours, you might be any shape, almost." Thus, Humpty, as a particular "egg" was defined by his resemblance to other "eggs" in being called by the same name. However, he could not determine how to reconcile, by resemblance, the particular "Alice" with the larger, universal group of "Alices."

Locke's empiricism attempted to build a system of thought exclusively from "the bottom up," abstracting observations only from particular phenomena while largely negating the validity of universal principles. The revived Platonic and Neoplatonic counter-reactions were guilty of the opposite extreme as they attempted to construct epistemologies from "the top down," deduced from purely *a priori* formulations. Berkeley's theory was also built from "the top down," but with an additional dependency upon God's perceiving mind. The mystic, as noted earlier, recognizes the wisdom in actively integrating the particular and the universal aspects of being, rather than attempting to build a system of thought exclusively from either "the top down" or from "the bottom up." Carroll's writings suggest that he advocated this combined method. In *Euclid, Book V, Proved Algebraically*, for example, Carroll utilized technical, formal symbolic manipulations to demonstrate the reliability of geometry as a pure science. Parallel lines or right angles exist as purely universal principles, but would never have been discovered without empirical experimentation. The value of the geometric figure lies in both its universal nature and the significance and usefulness of its particular applications. Through a creative dialectic between the temporal and the eternal, there occurs a form of integration between otherwise purely theoretic and pragmatic applications that gives practical substance to mysticism. The initiatory phases of Carroll's practical mysticism, revealed in the *Alice* books, come to maturity in the later *Sylvie and Bruno* books. Hidden behind Mock Turtles and March Hares, and concealed in places like Fairyland and Outland, Carroll's ultimate work-in-progress—the evolution of his own consciousness—is available, with some literary archaeology, to be showcased.

Alice

CHAPTER IV

The Muse behind the Mystic

TIME, SPACE, AND GRAVITY

$\mathcal{P}$eter Heath muses that *Alice in Wonderland* and *Through the Looking-Glass* "are works... whose frolics are governed... by a sometimes surprising insight into abstract questions of philosophy."[121] He fleshed out his observation by speculating that, although the earliest version of *Alice's Adventures* may have been extemporized by Carroll on the famous boat-trip, the "more characteristic details, plus the whole of *Through the Looking-Glass*, were meticulously elaborated in Dodgson's study in Christ Church."[122] Alvin L. Baum's essay, *Carroll's Alice: The Semantics of Paradox* adds,

---

121 Harold Bloom, ed. *Modern Critical Views: Lewis Carroll* (New York: Chelsea House Publishers, 1987), 46, citing Peter Heath, *The Philosopher's Alice* (New York: St. Martin's Press, 1974).
122 Ibid., 47.

likewise, "it is unreasonable to assume that he (Carroll) could have unwittingly composed a complete allegory."[123] Alexander L. Taylor, in *The White Knight*, chronicled that as age and social disappointments diminished Carroll's keenness, there was gain as well as loss. With reference to the *Alice* books, in which Carroll's message is so carefully obscured, Taylor states, "his most dynamic writings are his most obscure."[124] Taylor claimed that Carroll was not able to maintain this level of subtlety in *Sylvie and Bruno* where the philosophical themes appear blatantly obvious. With reference to Carroll's change in style and ability, Taylor writes, "As inspiration declined he became more explicit."[125] The *Sylvie and Bruno* books, written in the twilight of Carroll's life, with declining literary technique, supply obvious tools for understanding "what he was doing in the sixties when he gave nothing away."[126] Carroll delivered his final lecture, prior to his retirement from Oxford, on November 30, 1881. Only two students, out of a possible nine, were in attendance. Carroll made a diary entry that he "felt sad and old" although he was not yet fifty.[127] Declining powers, waning inspiration and growing eccentricity marked this part of his life. He was, in a sense, finished with the world and, yet, strangely as we shall see, still very much a part of it.

Gilbert Chesterton pointed to Carroll's prowess in writing the earlier *Alice* books by remarking, "it is not children who ought to read the words of Lewis Carroll—they are far better employed making mud-pies. Carroll's words should be read by sages and gray-haired philosophers... in order to study the

---

123 Bloom, *Modern Critical Views*, citing Alvin L. Baum, 68.
124 Alexander L. Taylor, *The White Knight: A Study of C.L. Dodgson (Lewis Carroll)* (Philadephia: Dufour Editions, 1963), vi.
125 Ibid.
126 Ibid.
127 Ibid., 176.

darkest problems of metaphysics, the borderland between reason and unreason, and the nature of the most erratic of spiritual forces, humour, which eternally dances between the two."[128] This view is strengthened by Carroll's own frequent admission that words could express meaning buried so deep in an author's mind that he himself or she herself may not always be consciously aware of them.

An approach to one of Carroll's most significant philosophical conundrums can be made by observing that the *Alice* books take place against a backdrop of temporal and spatial relationships and are rich in concerns about external space and time themes.[129] In the Neoplatonic tradition, the faded splendor of earthly existence was patterned in always-fluctuating time, which was itself only an imperfect copy of eternity. Everything in man's phenomenal existence was merely the shadowy image of the ideal Form. Plotinus conceptualized time as the movement of the reasoning faculty, which grasps one thought after another, and passes from one perception to another. It has no other existence than this. It is not, in the pure sense, to be confused with the successive changes of external things, such as the stars. These are in time, and rather than create time, they reveal it.[130] Therefore, while space is a fact of sensible existence, time is purely objective. Time embodies both the perpetual beginning and the perpetual ending. This, conceptually, points to the difficulty in making a clear distinction between "where "night"

---

128 Lewis Carroll, *The Hunting of the Snark*. Introduction by Martin Gardner. (London: Penguin Classics, 1998); Gardner citing Gilbert Chesterton ("The Library of the Nursery", *Lunacy and Letters,* 1958).

129 Phyllis Greenacre, *Swift and Carroll: A Psychoanalytic Study in Two Lives* (New York: International University Press, 1955), 173.

130 C. Bigg, *Chief Ancient Philosophies: Neoplatonism* (London: Society for Promoting Christian Knowledge, 1895), 212.

ends and "day" begins, which was one of Carroll's favourite topics. This subject is showcased in the story of the Mad Tea-Party where it is "always six o'clock." Arthur Stanley Eddington, in writing on relativity theory in *Space, Time and Gravitation*,[131] has compared the Mad Tea-Party to De Sitter's[132] model of the cosmos in which time stands eternally still. This concept was explored further when Alice questioned the seating rotations by asking, "What happens when you come to the beginning again?" Her inquiry is hastily dismissed when the March Hare interrupts, "Suppose we change the subject?" At this point, Carroll appears to be grappling with the absolute and relative aspects implicit in a doctrine of abstraction. From the absolute viewpoint, the universe is perceived in the nature of an illusion, a dream or phantasmagoria, as compared with the Forms themselves. Anything that has a beginning and an ending must be, in a sense, unreal and untrue. However, this absolute point of view shows only one side of the picture. The other side claims relative truths are those that can be understood by the limits of human understanding. From the relative viewpoint, that which is called *matter* exists to the senses as an aggregate of atoms, which are themselves merely a grouping of electrons, vibrating in constant motion. This position has us kick a stone and feel its impact. Although it seems to be real, we know that this is so only in a relative sense. Thus, it is folly to deny matter in the relative sense and equally foolish to admit it in the absolute sense.[133] This problem is resolved through the

---

131 Arthur Stanley Eddington, *Space, Time and Gravitation, An Outline of the General Relativity Theory* (Cambridge University Press, 1920).

132 Willem de Sitter, 1872-1934.

133 Three Initiates, *The Kybalion: A Study of the Hermetic Philosophy of Ancient Egypt and Greece* (Chicago: The Yogi Publication Society, 1908), 81.

Neoplatonic dualistic principle that opposites are only two extremes of the same thing, with many varying degrees between them. An inspection of a thermometer will not tell where "heat" terminates and "cold" begins, as a clear distinction between "absolute heat" and "absolute cold" is impossible within the confines of *a posteriori* experience.

Carroll, in his squib *Eight or Nine Words on Letter Writing,* made the point that, for example, "old" was a relative term. "I think you would be *quite* justified in addressing a chicken, just out of the shell, as 'old boy!' when compared with another chicken that was only half out!" penned Carroll.[134] This idea takes on numerous contexts throughout the *Alice* books. For example, the Red Queen's position is obvious when she says, "I've seen gardens, compared with which this would be a wilderness." She repeats the theme by stating, "I could show you hills, in comparison with which you'd call that a valley." Likewise, the relativity of beauty is touched upon in the wood by the Duchess' house when Alice observed that the baby-turned-pig "would have been a dreadfully ugly child; but it makes a rather handsome pig." Metaphysical speculations about the relativity of beauty continue in *Through the Looking-Glass* as Alice drifts by the scented rushes and cries, "Oh, what a lovely one! Only I couldn't quite reach it. And it certainly did seem a little provoking ('almost as if it happened on purpose,' she thought) that though she managed to pick plenty of beautiful rushes as the boat glided by, there was always a more lovely one that she couldn't reach." The dream rushes seem symbolic of the realm of Beauty beyond the sensible world that is, nonetheless, perceptible to the mind. The unattainable rushes were perceptible to Alice's eye, but were not within the reach of her sensory, tactile experience.

---

134 Stuart Dodgson Collingwood, *Life and Letters of Lewis Carroll* (New York: The Century Co., 1898), 277.

Carroll's addition of the parenthetical "almost as if it happened on purpose" reinforces this interpretation.

The absolute and relative senses of time are repeatedly contrasted, as well, in the *Alice* books. When, for example, Alice sees the White Rabbit rushing past with his little watch, and his "Oh dear! I shall be too late!" time is shown in a quantitative, relative light. Moments later Alice falls down the perpendicular rabbit-hole with the sensations of one who watches a slowed-down moving picture. In contrast to the Rabbit's situation where time is very sharply defined by an "o'clock," here time is separated from gravity, and has no quantitative properties.[135] Time was so devoid of beginning or ending that Alice was able to pick a jar of marmalade from a shelf and replace it on another one without interrupting the flow of her free-fall.

The eternal nature of absolute Time is hinted at when Alice recounts the history of her adventures to her sister, telling her about having sung *"Here we go round the mulberry bush."* "I don't know when I began it but somehow I felt as if I'd been singing it a long, long time!" In contrast, time in its relative sense is portrayed when Alice asks the King, "'Would you— be good enough'—, Alice panted out, after running a little further, 'to stop a minute—just to—get one's breath again?'" "'I'm good enough,' the King said, 'only I'm not strong enough. You see, a minute goes by so fearfully quick. You might as well try to stop a Bandersnatch.'" By punning the phrase "to stop a minute" in this particular syntax, Carroll was able to highlight the relative aspect of temporality.

This theme is explored more deeply when Alice remarks to the Mad Hatter, "What a funny watch! It... doesn't tell what o'clock it is!" "Why should it?" the Hatter answered, "Does your watch tell you what year it is?" Alice assured him that it

---

135 This consideration becomes especially important, as we shall see, when Carroll explores gravity.

certainly didn't since "it stays the same year for such a long time altogether." The Hatter confused Alice even more when he responded, "Which is just the case with mine." Time, merely an imperfect copy of eternity, having no real effect upon the enduring nature of reality, has no true linear properties. Time, in the physical realm, does not have absolute reality, but only relative existence so that the "o'clock" has no real significance on Time. Later in the party, the Hatter shares with Alice that time would "do almost anything you liked with the clock" on the condition that she "kept on good terms" with Time. The Hatter strengthens his position by illustrating, "suppose it were nine o'clock in the morning, just in time to begin lessons, you'd only have to whisper a hint to Time, and round goes the clock in a twinkling!" Here, Carroll portrays pure, absolute Time in contrast to the empirical unit of measure produced by the instrument of "the clock." The eternal properties of absolute Time have no beginnings and no endings, while the designations of "the clock" have no real or true existence. It is worth noting that Carroll, in this setting, penned "Time" with a "T". If, along with Plato, Carroll viewed time as an imperfect copy of eternity, then mankind, poised between relative and absolute time, or eternity, is engaged in a constant dialectic between the phenomenal, material realm and noumenal, immaterial experience.

We find Carroll himself irreconcilably, and probably unconsciously, suspended between the phenomenal and noumenal realms. During his academic tenure, interest began to dawn in differentiating a new theoretical physics from Newtonian physics, based on space being conceived of as n-dimensional, with time as its fourth dimension. The proponents of this theory[136] declared that it was impossible to completely isolate any existing object from the element of time and that the

136 The most prominent proponents of this theory were nineteenth-

failure to include this element destroys the congruity of the object under consideration. More specifically, some mathematical physicists discovered that experimental contradictions disappeared if, instead of referring to phenomena as a set of three-space axes and one-time axes, they referred to them as a set of four interchangeable axes involving four homogenous coordinates.[137] In other words, they used time as if it were a dimension of space. This would mean that space was four-dimensional which, of course, foreshadowed the theory of relativity. From the standpoint of general relativity, space-time was curved, predicated on interpretations extrapolated from non-Euclidean geometry. This mathematical possibility of a fourth dimension was slowly attaining acceptability, but with its entrance into physical theory the query inevitably arose as to what might be the objects corresponding to these higher dimensions. A difficulty arose from the fact that the conception of a four-dimensional object necessitated the assumption that it consisted of an infinite number of three-dimensional solids. For example, a cube consists of an infinite number of squares. A square, considered as a purely mathematical entity, having no physical existence, can be visualized as having no thickness, therefore making an infinite number of such squares conceivable. With the cube, however, the case is different, as the cube has physical reality. As a result of the mathematical possibility of a fourth dimension, though, the possibility of an infinite number of such cubes becomes conceivable.

Thus, at this point, Carroll's philosophical conundrum comes into focus. Carroll, interested in spiritualist phenomena and mystical experience, was also fiercely loyal to classical

---

century British mathematicians William Kingdon Clifford and Arthur Cayley.

137 Geoffry Hodson and Alexander Horne, *Some Experiments in Four Dimensional Vision* (London: Rider and Co., 1933), vi.

Euclidean principles. As the new theoretical physics budded, it began to supply preliminary evidence that could, eventually, have lent support to the possibilities of paranormal and mystical experience. At the same time, it did so by utilizing methodologies based on non-Euclidean geometry. Considering points of reconciliation between science and spirituality was untenable among the academic community of Victorian Oxford. It appears that Carroll, like most academics of this period, confused the map with the territory. The territory was the immaterial, while maps could be crafted by either science or spirituality. Due to his loyalty to Euclid, as well as his distrust of empirical science, Carroll apparently overlooked the possibility of new physics as an avenue for opening up a whole new integrated frontier. His apparent intrigue, for example, with the concept of time as the fourth dimension from a paranormal viewpoint, could not be reconciled with his distrust of the implications of the application of quaternions to geometry nor the resultant concept of a curved space-time, predicated on principles of non-Euclidean geometry.

In the introduction to *Sylvie and Bruno Concluded* Carroll refers to having read *Transcendental Physics*, an account of experimental investigations into spiritualist phenomena, by Johann Carl Friedrick Zöllner, Professor of Physics and Astronomy at the University of Leipzig. Carroll was also introduced to the work of Gustav Theodor Fechner, Professor of Physics at the University of Leipzig, through Max Müller. Müller came to Christ Church after a tenure at the University of Leipzig, bringing with him Fechner's books and his correspondence with Fechner.[138] Fechner, as did Carroll, published scholarly works in his academic field under his own name and imaginative literature under a pseudonym, Dr Mises. "Space has Four Dimensions" was one of the *Vier*

---

138 Taylor, *White Knight*, 89.

Paradoxe published by Fechner as Dr Mises in 1864. It was a mixture of science, philosophy and satire, very much after Carroll's own manner. In this work, Fechner-Mises proves that time is really a fourth dimension by the process of removing the other three. He imagines a small coloured figurine running around on the paper in a camera obscura and points out that such a being would know as little of the third, as we of the fourth, dimension. Yet, we allege the existence of the third. So, what is this fourth dimension? Fechner-Mises instructs his readers to imagine passing the animated figurine through the third dimension along a beam of light. "As it comes into other areas of light, it will itself be altered thereby and perhaps at the end of the way it will appear pale and wrinkled, whereas at the beginning it was smooth and round."[139] Fechner asserts that this process is time. This, says Fechner, is due to the movement of our space of three dimensions through the fourth, of which movement we perceive only the passage of time and the consequent change. At each moment we have a cross-section of this larger reality, of which as a whole we know nothing. Fechner's ideas were incongruent with Plotinus' theory that, in a pure sense, time was not to be confused with the successive changes of external things, in this case the movement of our space of three dimensions through a fourth. Whereas Fechner claimed that we perceive only the passage of time and the consequent change, Plotinus maintained that these successive changes of external things were in time, rather than creating time. Fechner, however, argues that if one follows this Neoplatonic conception of time, there is no reason why time should not run backward instead of forward, and the whole history of the world in reverse.

139 Ibid.

Carroll grapples with this theme in multiple settings throughout his *Alice* books. When Alice was straightening the Queen's shawl and the Queen offered to hire her for "twopence a week and jam every other day," she learned that "the rule is, jam to-morrow and jam yesterday—but never jam to-day." Confused, Alice responded, "I don't understand you," to which the Queen replied, "that's the effect of living backwards, it always makes one a little giddy at first." The Queen then cited the advantage of living backwards in that "one's memory works both ways," after which she boasted of being able to remember things that had not yet happened. Carroll portrays this theme even more fervently in Chapter 23 of *Sylvie and Bruno* with the invention of "the Outlandish Watch owned by the German professor." Setting the Outlandish Watch's hands back in time resulted in setting the events themselves back to the time indicated on the watch. Spinning off of Plato's *Statesman*, Carroll stages a scenario by which pressing a "reversal peg" on the Outlandish Watch would start events moving backwards.[140]

Time, similarly, stands still as Alice and the Red Queen ran, hand in hand, at an ever accelerating pace. As the Queen shouted "Faster! Faster!" Alice noticed "that the trees and other things round them never changed their places at all: however fast they went, they never seemed to pass anything." When they finally paused to rest, Alice exclaimed in astonishment, "Why, I do believe we've been under this tree the whole time! Everything's just as it was!" In this scene, unlike Fechner, Carroll gives credence to Plotinus' conceptualization of time as the movement of the reasoning faculty, whereby time grasps one thought after another, and passes one perception after another, without having any relationship with successive changes in external things. This

---

140 Martin Gardner, *The Annotated Alice* (New York: Clarkson N. Potter, Inc., 1960), 96.

particular Carrollian scenario also hints at the inter-relationship between time and motion, and the philosophical problems implicit in it.

It is likely that Carroll was familiar with Sir William Rowan Hamilton's *Lectures on Quaternions* (1852), where the introductory remarks share territorial congruence with Fechner-Mises in viewing time as a dimension.[141] Hamilton's map, however, indicated that expressions which had hitherto been regarded as symbolic might acquire reality and signifi-cance if algebra were viewed in a pure sense, that is, as the science of order in progression, rather than merely the com-putation of quantity. The application of quaternions to geometry was controversial in the late 1800s. While quaternions provided superior notation for four dimensions, they could not be used with arbitrary dimensionality. William Kingdon Clifford, influenced by the work of Riemann and Lobachevsky, generalized quaternions to what he called biquaternions and used them to study motion in non-Euclidean spaces. In 1870, he wrote *On the Space Theory of Matter* in which he argued that energy and matter are simply different types of curvature of space. In this work Clifford presented ideas that were to form a fundamental role in Einstein's general theory of relativity. While it is generally accepted that Clifford's ideas were untenable in the 1870s, attitudes within the academic community changed so dramatically in the intervening years that nearly the same concepts were tenable during Einstein's early career. Two generations of thinkers who expressed an interest in the non-Euclidean geometries and hyperspaces separated Clifford's original work from general relativity. During that time, the popularity of physical interpretations of the non-Euclidean geometries grew. However, during Carroll's tenure, physical

141 Taylor, *White Knight*, 92.

interpretations of the non-Euclidean geometries were, for the most part, still considered geometrical heresy.

Carroll, representing this traditional Victorian academic position, wrote in the Preface to the First Edition of *Euclid and His Modern Rivals* about "the great cause which I have at heart—the vindication of Euclid's masterpiece." Loyalty to Euclid during this period was based on a conviction of the absolute nature of his propositions. Today, it is difficult to fathom that only one hundred years ago, Professors Arthur Cayley of Cambridge and W. K. Clifford of London "may well have been the only Englishmen who understood the philosophical revolution that had been instigated by Gauss, Bolyai and Lobachevsky,[142] some 50 or 60 years earlier."[143] Cayley, possibly the staunchest advocate of Euclidean three-dimensionality, even while a friend, teacher and colleague of Clifford's, eventually became swayed by Clifford's arguments. This admission demonstrated a crack in the thick veneer shrouding both Cayley's and the Victorian dedication to Euclideanism since Cayley was the inventor of a mathematical system, the projective geometry, which offered the only logical alternative to the radical concept of a curved space. Here we see the first cracks in the steadfast pillar of Victorian geometry. It is interesting to speculate what might have transpired if either Cayley or Clifford had met Dodgson and convinced him that there was a logically consistent non-Euclidean, hyperbolic geometry in which the absolute nature of the propositions of Table I still held, even though the statements in Table II were false.[144] This speculation is especially provocative in light of the fact that twenty-first

---

142 C. F. Gauss (1777-1855), N. Lobachevsky (1793-1856), J. Bolyai (1802-1860), and B. Riemann (1826-1846) are traditionally associated with the discovery of non-Euclidean geometries.

143 Charles L. Dodgson, *Euclid and His Modern Rivals,* Introduction by H. S. M. Coxeter (New York: Dover Publications, Inc., 1973), vii.

144 Ibid.

century quantum physics, sharing multiple points of reconciliation with spiritual mysticism,[145] leans toward accepting a four-dimensional reality demonstrated by hyperbolic principles.[146]

The concept of the absolute nature of Euclid's propositions, though popular among Victorian academics, would not have found favour, either, with concurrent Berkeleyian trends that were also competing for favour in nineteenth century England. Dissonance would have arisen from the concept of the absolute nature of Euclid's propositions having been founded on a doctrine of abstraction. Berkeley had a very concrete notion of time, as a train of successive ideas, which appeared often in the *Philosophical Commentaries*, and was contrasted with Newtonian or abstract time in *Principles,* 97-8. Berkeley denied the infinite divisibility of time, as of space, opposing it to his own conception of indivisible sensible points or *minima.* Berkeley argued against Newton, that all observed motions were relative, as was all observed rest. He went so far as to say that there were no absolutes at all within the realm of

---

145 See Fritjof Capra's *The Tao of Physics* (Boston: Shambhala Publications, Inc., 1975); Gary Zukav's *The Dancing Wu Li Masters* (New York: Harper Collins Publishers, Inc., 1979), and/or William Arntz's *What the Bleep Do We Know!?* (Deerfield Beach, Florida: Health Communications, Inc., 2005).

146 Recently, there has been some renewed interest in the relationship between Clifford's theory and its role in the development of modern physics. Ruth Farwell and Christopher Knee ("The End of the Absolute: A Nineteenth Century Contribution to General Relativity," *Studies in the History and Philosophy of Science,* March 1990, 21: 91-121) have looked at Clifford's work as a "nineteenth century contribution to general relativity." Joan Richards, in *Mathematical Visions: The Pursuit of Geometry in Victorian England,* (Boston: Harcourt Brace Jovanovitch, 1988) likewise, has written on the development of non-Euclidean geometry in Victorian England, a movement in which Clifford played a significant role.

physics.[147] The concept of absolute, as well as relative, time, motion and space, claimed Berkeley, wrongly supposed that those qualities could exist without mind. Berkeley asserted that we must distinguish between mathematical hypotheses and natures of things. Terms such as *gravity* do not denote physical or metaphysical entities. They are merely mathematical hypotheses. Mechanics cannot progress without the use of mathematical abstractions and hypotheses, so their use is, thus, justified by their practical utility. However, the practical usefulness of a mathematical abstraction does not prove that it denotes any physical or metaphysical reality. According to Berkeley, metaphysics must be eliminated from physics and the two should not be confused.

These concepts posed some problems for Carroll, as well, but his solution was quite different than Berkeley's. As a Victorian geometer, Carroll viewed mathematics as providing a base of absolute truths to physics. In the Newtonian theory of gravitation, space and time were the stage upon which physical processes were displayed. In these processes the masses were acting directly upon each other. As the evolution toward theories of relativity developed, however, space and time began to be seen as fused together in a continuum called space-time. The geometrical properties of this space-time determined the evolution of the physical processes in space and time. It was thought that the masses and physical processes present in space and time determined the geometrical properties of the space-time continuum. As this thinking developed, nothing was viewed as external or uninfluenced, and the series of causes of mechanical phenomena became closed. The geometrical properties of space-time were concluded to be functions of a four-dimensional continuum.

---

147 A. D. Ritchie, *George Berkeley: A Reappraisal* (New York: Barnes and Noble, Inc., 1967), 88.

This evolutionary trajectory, therefore, eliminated the concept of gravitational forces. The guidance of particles did not take place by a direct interaction between them, but was accomplished by the geometrical structure of space and time. As this theory matured, gravitational forces, in the Newtonian sense, arose only if we refused to properly interpret the geometry of space-time.

Carroll's deliberate integration of gravity issues into both the *Alice* and *Sylvie and Bruno* books imply the dissonance created by his refusal to eliminate metaphysics from physics, as Berkeley had suggested, while concomitantly dismissing non-Euclidean geometry. When Lady Muriel of *Sylvie and Bruno* remarks in astonishment about the "cups of tea having no weight at all," Arthur matter-of-factly asserts that, "one can imagine things having no weight." Here, Carroll's interest in psychic research, on one hand, would be resonant with the absence of gravity; while, on the other hand, his loyalty to Victorian geometry would have dismissed the concept of a continuum of space-time. The same material vexed him as Alice browsed in the old Sheep's little dark shop. Every time that Alice tried to examine a ware on the shelf, it floated up to a higher shelf. Plaintively, she said, "things flow about so here!" after having "spent a minute or so in vainly pursuing a large bright thing." She decided to "follow it up to the very top shelf of all," when the object "went through the ceiling as quietly as possible, as if it were quite used to it."

Although the effect of precursory relativity theory was to re-establish physics on a philosophical basis, the emerging empirical science was determined to ignore the metaphysical question and to accept only *experience* as the object of study. In support of this argument, it was emphasized, for example, that Galileo discovered the law of falling bodies by measuring how the space covered varied with the time of the fall. By carrying out certain processes of measurement, he obtained results that stood in a certain relation to one another, and remained thus, irrespective of what metaphysical status was, or was not, assigned to motion. Carroll's description of Alice's descent down the rabbit-hole suggests his reaction to this position. The issue of the space covered relative to the time of the fall was clearly intended to bear the brunt of Carrollian satire as Alice noted that "either the well was very deep, or she fell very slowly, for she had plenty of time as she went down to look about her, and to wonder what was going to happen next." "She took down a jar from one of the shelves as she passed" and then "managed to put it into one of the cupboards as she fell past it." Thus, Alice defied the law of falling bodies as she replaces the jar on a shelf without any de-acceleration of her free fall. Carroll focuses on this same issue again in Chapter 8 of *Sylvie and Bruno,* as he describes the difficulty of having tea inside a falling house, as well as being pulled downward at an even faster acceleration; unwittingly anticipating in some respects the "thought experiment" in which Einstein used an "imaginary falling elevator to explain certain aspects of relativity theory.[148] Alice's fall, although reported as having gone on for an excessively long time and through an extraordinarily long space, did not result in any physical injury. Thus, it must be concluded that there was no impact, although she landed on a heap of sticks and dry leaves, thereby mocking the principle of *experience* as the object of study.

Carroll parrots the Cambridge Platonists' criticisms of Galileo in his parody of the White Knight. When Alice asked the Knight if he had "invented a plan for keeping the hair from being blown off," he replied that he had not. However, he did have "a plan for keeping it from falling off." The Knight explained that "you take an upright stick, then you make your

---

148 Gardner, *Annotated Alice*, 27.

hair creep up it, like a fruit-tree." He continued that "the reason hair falls off is because it hangs down—things never fall upwards, you know." It must be noted that Carroll was specific in saying that the hair "crept upwards" as opposed to being "styled" or "held" upwards. Since its movement on the stick was upwards, the Knight felt justified in concluding that any fall that it might take would subsequently have to be in the same direction. Thus, the purely physical thrust of the Galilean law of "falling bodies", as well as the work that was based on his foundation, was taken to task.

The metaphysical problems implicit in any discussion of temporal and spatial relations become exacerbated as soon as motion is introduced. For, the problem of time reasserts itself concurrent with the admission of motion, since motion is inconceivable without time. The only escape from the enigma is to assert that any motion, even of consciousness, is itself an illusion, and that there is no real motion at all. For Berkeley, space and time were attributes of God, but not substantial or absolute, as Newton had claimed. Berkeley, thus, asserted that spatial and temporal relations were public and, therefore, universally available to all persons so as to form a single system. He further claimed that spatial and temporal relations were as phenomenal, for example, as the simple qualities of sense.[149] Plotinus, coming from a different perspective, maintained that time was only the movement of the reasoning faculty. Life, then, was a dream, and in this dream, we dream that we dream. Carroll characterized this perspective with reference to the Red King's dream. As Alice awoke from her *Looking-Glass* dream, she pondered the "serious question" of "who it was that dreamed it all." She queried, "it must have been either me or the Red King. He was part of my dream, of course—but then I was part of his dream, too!" So, an infinite

---

149 Ritchie,*George Berkeley*, 177.

regression is established between the dreams of Alice and those of the Red King. Alice dreams of the King, who is dreaming of Alice, who is dreaming of the King, and so forth.[150]

These dream motifs are especially important, as they reappear in Carroll's explorations of Platonism, Neoplatonism, Gnosticism and Cartesianism. As interesting as these other philosophical areas are with respect to Carroll, nothing is as provocative as the issues surrounding time, space and gravity. It is in this area alone that we come face-to-face with Carroll's conflict between his mysticism and his allegiance to the collective classical academic consciousness. This conflict, harder to identify in the other areas of exploration, portrays a man divided—a man who was very much in this world and, yet, strangely, not quite of it.

PLATONISM, NEOPLATONISM, AND GNOSTICISM

*T*he corpus of Greek writings attributed to Hermes Trismegistus and often quoted as the *Poimandres* is regarded as a prime document of independent pagan Gnosticism. Concurrent with Victorian England's revival of interest in Platonic and Neoplatonic thought, there was, concurrently, a resurgence of Gnostic themes in literature. To the poet, writer or artist of romantic or mystical temperament, Neoplatonism and Gnosticism walked hand-in-hand, teaching that there was a realm of Beauty beyond the sensible world

---

150 Gardner, *Annotated Alice*, 238.

that was perceptible to the mind. J. A. Stewart, in *Platonism and the English Poets,* wrote:

> Platonism I would describe, in the most general terms, as the mood of one who has a curious eye for the endless variety of this visible and temporal world and a fine sense of its beauties, yet is haunted by the presence of an invisible and eternal world behind, or, when the mood is most pressing, within, the visible and temporal world, and sustaining both it and himself—a world not perceived as external to himself, but inwardly, lived by him, as that with which, at moments of ecstasy, or even habitually, he is become one.[151]

Gnostic themes, in Victorian literature, maintained a radical dualism that polarized the whole existence of reality. Every thesis had an implicit antithesis. On one hand, there was spirit; on the other, matter. Likewise, body and soul, light and dark, good and evil, life and death. Carroll's *Alice* books abound with dualism. Almost everything is presented in terms of an opposite. The opening sentence of *Through the Looking-Glass* is Alice's charge that "one thing is certain, that the *white* kitten had had nothing to do with it—it was the *black* kitten's fault entirely." Two pages later, Carroll confronts us with the difference between damnation and grace. Alice has barely mused, "Suppose they saved up all my *punishments*? What would they do at the end of the year?" when she suddenly hears the snow against the windowpanes and says, "I wonder if the snow *loves* the trees and fields, it kisses them so gently?"

Some of Carroll's dual images are obvious, like Tweedledee and Tweedledum's "contrariwise," while others are woven more subtly into the fabric of the text. In *Through the Looking-Glass,* the chapter entitled *Humpty Dumpty* features an egg who sits in perfect balance on a wall and never falls, while the

---

151 John Gregory, *The Neoplatonists* (London: Kyle Cathie Ltd., 1991), 249.

very next chapter, *The Lion and the Unicorn*, features a group of soldiers so imbalanced that Alice "had never seen soldiers so uncertain on their feet: they were always tripping over something or other... and it seemed to be a regular rule that, whenever a horse stumbled, the rider fell off instantly." This type of literary device, presenting a dualistic relationship of man and the world, is consistent with Gnostic thought.

According to the Gnostic tradition, the universe is like a vast prison whose innermost dungeon is the material earth, the scene of man's life. This scene is enacted in what is referred to as the chaotic space "underneath". Alice's transport to Wonderland was "Down, down, down" the rabbit hole. "Down, down, down. Would the fall *never* come to an end?" Interestingly, Carroll had originally named the story *Alice's Adventures Underground*. It was not until June 18, 1864 that he finally decided upon *Alice's Adventures in Wonderland*. Likewise, the journey into the Looking-glass House was similar. "'Oh, Kitty, how nice it would be if we could only get through into Looking-glass House!... Let's pretend the glass has got all soft like gauze, so that we can get through. Why, it's turning into a sort of mist now, I declare! It'll be easy enough to get through—.' She was up on the chimney-piece while she said this, although she hardly knew how she got there... In another moment Alice was through the glass, and had jumped lightly down into the Looking-glass room." Both "underneath" points of arrival, Wonderland and Looking-glass House, were the scenes of chaos. This is one of the fundamental symbols of Gnosticism. A pre-cosmic fall of part of the divine principle underlies the genesis of human existence.

Gnosticism further claims that the spirit, in its immersion in the material body, is unconscious of itself, benumbed, asleep, intoxicated by the poison of the world. In brief, it is ignorant. Its awakening and liberation is affected by "knowledge." In the Gnostic context, "knowledge" (*gnosis*) has an emphatically religious meaning and refers to the objects of faith (*pistis*). Pre-eminently, gnosis meant the knowledge of Divine Nature. This motif was a critical component in both *Wonderland* and *Looking-Glass* with Alice awakening, at the conclusion of each, from "a most curious dream." In both books, Alice's awakening and liberation occurs when she arrives at a piece of "knowledge"—that all of the poems are about fish![152] Christian writings have historically used the symbol of the fish to represent Christ as the object of faith. Thus, it could be interpreted that Alice arrives at a "knowledge" of Divine Nature.

The goal of Gnostic striving is the release of the individual from the bonds of the chaotic material world and their return to his or her native realm of light. At this time of release, the individual's spiritual morality is established by hostility toward the material world and its mundane ties.[153] Alice's release from the bonds of *Wonderland* was enacted in a moment of hostility toward the Queen of Hearts and her government. "'No, no!', said the Queen. 'Sentence first—verdict afterwards.' 'Stuff and nonsense!' said Alice loudly. 'The idea of having the sentence first!' 'Hold your tongue', said the Queen, turning purple. 'I won't!', said Alice. 'Off with her head!' the Queen shouted at the top of her voice. 'Who cares for *you?*' said Alice (she had grown to her full size by this time). 'You're nothing but a pack of cards!' At this the whole pack... came flying down upon her... and she tried to beat them off, and found herself lying on the bank, with her head in the lap of her sister....." This theme of liberation through hostile rejection is even more developed in *Looking-*

---

152 Donald J. Gray, ed. *Authoritative Texts of Alice in Wonderland/ Through the Looking-Glass/Hunting of the Snark: Backgrounds and Essays in Criticism* (New York: W.W. Norton and Co., 1992), 348.
153 Jonas, *Gnostic Religion*, 46.

Glass, as the book concludes with Alice's cry, "I can't stand this any longer!" as she pulled up the table-cloth and sent plates, dishes, guests and candles crashing to the floor.

A popular Gnostic literary image was that of "the alien." The alien is one who originates elsewhere and does not belong in the material world. To the alien, the material world is a foreign land that is strange, unfamiliar, and incomprehensible. Thus, the alien suffers the lot of the stranger who is lonely and unprotected in a situation fraught with danger. The stranger does not know the ways of the foreign land and wanders about lost.[154] Alice was "the alien" or the stranger in both Wonderland and the Looking-glass House. In both instances, she had originated in a land "above." When she made her respective falls into Wonderland and the Looking-glass House, she found both realms strange, unfamiliar and incomprehensible. Time was distorted; gravitational influences, altered.

Linguistic and mathematical structures were challenged, and the available objects of perception were different from those in her previous experience. Likewise, both places "underneath" were filled with danger. She risked drowning in a pool of tears, being decapitated by the Queen's executioners, and shrinking away into extinction. Not knowing the ways of either Wonderland or the Looking-glass World, Alice often wandered about lost. An example is given when Alice gingerly asked, "Cheshire-Puss, … would you tell me, please, which way I ought to go from here?" The Cat, amplifying Alice's disorientation, replied that it "depended a great deal on where you want to get to." The theme of Alice as the lost stranger is explicit in the opening lines of "The Garden of Live Flowers." "'I should see the garden far better,' said Alice to herself, 'if I could get to the top of that hill: and here's a path that leads

---

154 Ibid., 49.

straight to it—at least, no it doesn't do that—' (after going a few yards along the path, and turning several sharp corners), 'but I suppose it will at last. But how curiously it twists! It's more like a corkscrew than a path! Well this turn goes to the hill, I suppose—no, it doesn't! This goes straight back to the house! Well then, I'll try it the other way.' And she did: wandering up and down, and trying turn after turn, but always coming back to the house...." These lines paint a clear picture of Alice being lost and unable to find her way. They also, however, highlight another image that is used frequently in Gnostic myth and allegory: the image of the material world as a "dwelling" or "house." This theme is easily seen in *Through the Looking-Glass* with its emphasis on the Looking-glass House. "'But oh!' thought Alice, suddenly jumping up, 'if I don't make haste, I shall have to go back through the Looking-glass, before I've seen what the rest of the house is like! Let's have a look at the garden first!'"

Carroll appears to utilize another popular Gnostic image in *The Lion and the Unicorn*. Alice, about to answer the Lion, was interrupted by a deafening din. "But before Alice could answer him, the drums began. Where the noise came from, she couldn't make out: the air seemed full of it, and it rang through and through her head till she felt quite deafened." It was popular in Gnostic literature to use the "noise of the world" as a literary image. The noise of the material world drowns out the "call of life" and deafens man to the voice of the alien.[155]

Interwoven into what appears to be Carroll's Gnostic imagery, there are also subtle suggestions of Platonism and Neoplatonism. The ancient Neoplatonists regarded matter as the parent of ignorance, believing that, due to their inferior status, material objects could not co-exist with consciousness.

---

155 Ibid., 68.

Material objects were the confusing, limiting, inhibiting and imprisoning parts of existence. Neoplatonic interpretation of Plato's theory of the Forms emphasized the material world's distance from, rather than likeness to, reality. The mirror was a favourite device for illustrating this concept, signifying that there exists an Eternal World where the Permanent Realities of everything that is seen in the mirror, or material world, exist. The images that are reflected in the mirror are distorted and broken, mere shadows of this Eternal World. Therefore, the idea of material objects as real and true is ludicrous, being only shadows falling upon shadow as in a mirror where the position of the apparent is different from that of the real object.[156] By definition, a looking glass is a mirror. Hence, the first clue for systematizing Carroll's philosophy in his literary setting of *Through the Looking-Glass* is given. It is worth noting that the contemporary idea of a holographic paradigm is essentially a re-statement of Neoplatonic views. Prime architects of this idea were University of London's David Bohm, a protégé of Einstein's and one of the world's most respected quantum physicists; and Karl Pribram, a neuro-physiologist at Stanford University and author of the classical neuropsychological textbook, *Languages of the Brain*. The holographic paradigm is a perspective that sees that the world and everything in it as mere projections from a level of reality existing beyond space and time.[157] In 1984, when John P. Briggs and F. David Peat wrote a book (New York: Simon and Schuster) about the cosmos as a hologram, they entitled it *Looking-Glass Universe!*

---

156 Kathleen Raine and George Mills Harper, *Thomas Taylor The Platonist: Selected Writings* (Princeton: Princeton University Press, 1969), 79.

157 Michael Talbot, *The Holographic Universe* (New York: Harper Perennial, 1992), 1.

Martin Gardner cites Fredric Brown's *Night of the Jabberwock* as a source suggesting that Carroll was interested in these themes. Brown's narrator is an enthusiastic Carrollian who learns from a man calling himself Yehudi Smith, apparently a member of a society of Carroll admirers called The Vorpal Blades, "that Carroll's fantasies are not fiction at all, but realistic reporting about another plane of existence. The clues to the fantasies are cleverly concealed in Carroll's mathematical treatises, especially *Curiousa Mathematica,* and in his non-acrostic poems, which are really acrostics of a subtler kind."[158]

Carroll's satirization of sensory experience, with its dependence upon physical sensation, goes hand-in-hand with Gnostic, Platonic and Neoplatonic themes. The unreliability of sight for validating knowledge is illustrated in the interactions between Alice and the Red King. Alice noted the King's very slow climb up unto the table by stating, "'Why, you'll be hours and hours getting to the table, at that rate. I'd far better help you, hadn't I?' But the King took no notice of the question: it was quite clear that he could neither hear nor see her." Although she was neither visible nor audible, Carroll assures that she still retained a full command of her physical prowess, therefore confirming the reality of her existence. For, as Alice helped him up onto the table, "the King found himself held in the air by an invisible hand." "'Oh, please, don't make such faces, my dear?' she cried out, quite forgetting that the King couldn't hear her." Carroll drives his point home by having Alice, imperceptible to the senses, demonstrate the reality of her existence by moving the end of the King's pencil with such strength that he could not overcome her. "Alice looked on with great interest as the King took an enormous memorandum-

---

158 Martin Gardner, ed., *The Annotated Alice* (New York: Clarkson N. Potter, Inc., 1960), 194.

book out of his pocket, and began writing. A sudden thought struck her, and she took hold of the end of the pencil, which came some way over his shoulder, and began writing for him. The poor King... struggled with the pencil, but Alice was too strong for him...". Sensory experience is again taken to task, this time with a pun, when Humpty Dumpty recites his poem to Alice. "'In winter, when the fields are white, I sing this song for your delight—only I don't sing it,' he added, as an explanation. 'I see you don't,' said Alice. 'If you can *see* whether I'm singing or not, you've sharper eyes than most,' Humpty Dumpty remarked." Carroll continues to play out this theme when the King, in looking for the Messengers, instructs Alice, "'Just look along the road, and tell me if you can see either of them.' 'I see nobody on the road,' said Alice. 'I only wish I had such eyes... to be able to see Nobody! And at that distance, too!'" This quip is probably aimed at Berkeley. In explaining judgements of distance, Berkeley argued that what one sees, "the immediate objects of sight," are not things in space at a distance, but ideas of the mind. When one says that what one sees is a mile away, one must mean that were one to move forward a mile, one would be "affected with such and such ideas of touch".[159]

Carroll continues to entertain the frailty of sensory experience when the Unicorn says to Alice, "Well, now that we've seen each other... if you believe in me, I'll believe in you." It is possible that the Unicorn is suggesting that their mutual visual experience could provide satisfactory criteria for knowledge of one another's real and true existence. A few pages later, however, it is demonstrated that visual experience could not be trusted to provide a satisfactory criteria for knowledge of a thing's real and true existence. All of a sudden,

---

159 R. S. Woolhouse, *The Empiricists* (Oxford: Oxford University Press, 1988), 116.

"all sorts of things happened in a moment. The candles all grew up to the ceiling... as to the bottles, they each took a pair of plates, which they hastily fitted on as wings....at this moment, Alice heard a hoarse laugh at her side, but....instead of the Queen, there was the leg of mutton, sitting in a chair. 'Here I am,' cried a voice from the soup-tureen, and Alice turned again just in time to see the Queen's broad good-natured face grinning at her for a moment over the edge of the tureen, before she disappeared into the soup... as the soup ladle was walking up the table towards Alice's chair...." Here, experience is reduced to sensationalism and Plato's position from the *Theaetetus,* that sense perception is not knowledge, is affirmed. Since knowledge, for the Platonist, must satisfy the conditions of being real, stable and unchanging, none of these sense perceptions could provide Alice with knowledge. If we go back and look carefully at the wording of the Unicorn's claims, we will note that he said, "if you'll *believe* in me, I'll *believe* in you." Although the syntax was constructed in such a way as to imply that sensory experience of one another would allow Alice and the Unicorn to know that they co-existed, Carroll cleverly maintained that the most they could do would be to have a *belief* in one another's existence. Knowledge, as opposed to belief, must be real, stable and unchanging. Thus, the world of our sense experiences cannot satisfy the criteria of knowledge. This theme was repeated throughout the *Alice* books, as, for example, the characters were constantly changing size, the Duchess' baby turned into a pig, and the Cheshire-Cat materialized and dematerialized incessantly.

Dematerialization was a prominent theme throughout Carroll's imaginative literature and further pointed up the problems associated with attempting to establish knowledge through sensory experiences of material objects. When the two Queens had fallen asleep on Alice's lap at the close of *Through the Looking-Glass,* "the two great heads suddenly vanished..." thereby making sensory experience of the two Queens impossible. Alice had been rehearsed for this experience by an earlier disappearance of the Red Queen. "How it happened, Alice never knew, but exactly as she came to the last peg, she was gone. Whether she vanished into the air, or whether she ran quickly into the wood... there was no way of guessing, but she was gone." If, as was suggested, she "vanished into the air," then knowledge of the Queen was not possible since there was no available sense-perception of her material being.

Carroll's most developed material regarding this theme occurs with the Cheshire-Cat. Cudworth,[160] in his *Treatise Concerning Eternal and Immutable Morality,* identified two kinds of "perceptive cognitions" in the soul. One of these kinds is the active perceptions that arise from the mind itself without the body, and are called "conceptions of the mind." These virtually innate ideas are imprinted on the human mind by God. It is through these that we come to know both material and immaterial objects and truths.[161] Alice knew, for example, the Cheshire-Cat by a *conception of the mind.* When Alice was first introduced to him in the Duchess' kitchen, he was a material object, perceived as a "large cat, which was lying on the hearth grinning from ear to ear." However, in subsequent interactions with the cat, Alice did not have to

---

160 Ralph Cudworth (1617-1688) deserves recognition as one of the most important English seventeenth-century philosophers after Hobbes and Locke. In opposition to Hobbes, Cudworth proposes a theory of knowledge that may be contrasted with the empirical position of his younger contemporary Locke, and in moral philosophy he anticipates the ethical rationalists of the eighteenth century. *A Treatise Concerning Eternal and Immutable Morality* is his most important work.

161 Frederick Copleston, *The History of Philosophy,* vol. 5, ed. Edmund F. Sutcliffe (Westminster, Maryland: The Newman Press, 1959), 61.

perceive his material being in order to *know* him. As she was trying to find a way to escape the Queen's croquet game, "she noticed a curious appearance in the air: it puzzled her very much at first, but after watching it a minute or two she made it out to be a grin, and she said to herself 'It's the Cheshire-Cat: now I shall have somebody to talk to.'" All that was available to Alice's sense of perception was "a grin." However, since she knew the Cheshire-Cat by a conception of the mind, Alice was able to identify him in his immaterial state.

We see Carroll's satire again in force as Humpty Dumpty takes up nominalism,[162] that is, the view that universal terms do not refer to objective existences but are nothing more than *flatus vocis*—verbal utterances. Humpty Dumpty, in fact, subscribed to an extreme form of nominalism, according to which all that is common to a group of particulars is their being called by the same name. Humpty, as a particular *egg* was defined by his resemblance to other *eggs* by the same name. However, he could not determine how to reconcile, by resemblance, the particular *Alice* with the larger, universal group of *Alices*. This particular satire is probably aimed at either Berkeley's or Hobbes' nominalism.

Carroll extends his satire of Berkeley into "the woods of no names." We are reminded of Berkeley's contention that there were no such things as *abstract general ideas*. His view was that "an idea, which considered in itself is particular, becomes general by being made to represent all other particular ideas of the same sort."[163] Thus, universality does not consist "in

---

162 Nominalism is best understood in contrast to realism. Philosophical realism holds that when we use descriptive terms such as "green" or "tree," the Forms of those concepts really exist, independently of the world in an abstract realm. Such thought is associated with Plato, for instance. Nominalism, by contrast, holds that ideas represented by words have no real existence beyond our imaginations.

163 Copleston, *History of Philosophy*, vol. 5, 215.

the absolute, positive nature or conception of anything, but in the relation it bears to particulars signified or represented by it."[164] Since his view allows no abstract general ideas, it follows that reasoning must be about particulars. Berkeley does not, however, deny that there are *general words*. He, however, rejects Locke's theory that general words denote general ideas, if this is interpreted to mean that ideas possess a positive universal content. A proper name, such as Humpty Dumpty, signifies a plurality of things of a certain kind. Its universality, according to Berkeley, is a matter of use or function. Once this is established, we are spared the task of hunting for elusive entities that correspond to general words. Carroll seems to aim his satire at this position when the Gnat tells Alice that "Further on, in the wood down there, they've got no names—". Alice, upon entering this wood said, "'I mean to get under the—under the—this, you know!' putting her hand on the trunk of the tree. 'What does it call itself, I wonder? I do believe it's got no name—'". The general word in this instance would have been "tree." However, the general word is never assigned to the particular, satirizing Berkeley's claim of being "spared the task of hunting for elusive entities that correspond to general words."

Carroll's own view is found in the text of his book, *Symbolic Logic,* when he states that "... I maintain that any writer of a book is fully authorized in attaching any meaning he likes to any word or phrase he intends to use. If I find an author saying, at the beginning of his book, 'Let it be understood that by the word *"black"* I shall always mean *"white,"* and that by the word *"white"* I shall always mean *"black,"'* I merely accept his ruling, however injudicious I may think it."[165]

---

164 Ibid., 216.
165 Martin Gardner, *Annotated Alice*, 268-269.

Nominalism is again the theme when the Pigeon, thinking that Alice was a serpent, said "You're a serpent, and there's no use denying it. I suppose you'll be telling me next that you never tasted an egg!" Alice replied, "I have tasted eggs, certainly, but little girls eat eggs quite as much as serpents do, you know." To this bit of news, the Pigeon replied "... if they do... then they're a kind of serpent." Whereas the universals are defined in terms of resemblance, the eating of eggs, the particulars are required to resemble each other in being called by the same name, "serpents."

The final chapter of *Wonderland* is called "Alice's Evidence" and the subtitle of *Through the Looking-Glass* is "What Alice Found There." Both titles underscore the idea that Alice gains the evidence necessary to impel her to end her captivity in materialism. Any Victorian Churchman who had been introduced to Broad Church views would, whether consciously or unconsciously, naturally associate the title "Alice's Evidence" with William Paley's celebrated *Evidences (Natural Theology, or Evidence of the Existence and Attributes of the Deity Collected from the Appearances of Nature*, 1802)[166]. Paley's work, usually referred to simply as "Paley's Evidences," served during much of the nineteenth century as one of the principle sources for a proof of God's existence from

---

166 William Paley's (1743-1805) most influential contribution was *Natural Theology: or, Evidences of the Existence and Attributes of the Deity, Collected from the Appearances of Nature*, first published in 1802. In this book, Paley laid out a full exposition of natural theology, the belief that the nature of God could be understood by reference to His creation, the natural world. He introduced one of the most famous metaphors in the philosophy of science, the image of the watchmaker: "when we come to inspect the watch, we perceive... that its several parts are framed and put together for a purpose, e.g. that they are so formed and adjusted as to produce motion, and that motion so regulated as to point out the hour of the day; that if the different parts had been differently shaped from

the orderly design imposed upon natural phenomena. Among Victorian intellectuals, Paley's *Evidences* suffered an almost fatal blow from the empirical "evidences" presented by modern evolutionary theory.[167]

In his essay, *"The Child as Swain,"* William Empson[168] states that while *"Wonderland* is a dream, *Looking-Glass* is self-consciousness."[169] Carroll's treatment of myth and allegory points to Neoplatonic doctrines of spiritual harmony and interdependence of the universe. Carroll can be seen as singing harmony to Plotinus by suggesting that the whole hierarchy of spiritual reality exists within the individual soul. The *Alice* books reflect this influence as they invite an exploration of the self in its complexity, the causes of its alienation and disharmony, and the means of its liberation from rank materialism. Congruence with Neoplatonic and Gnostic doctrines is found in Carroll's theme of mankind's need to detach the immaterial soul from the corporeal body and external existence, and to turn inwards.

Though in the mind doth still abide: That is by Intellect supplied, And within that Idea doth hide: And he, that yearns

---

what they are, or placed after any other manner or in any other order than that in which they are placed, either no motion at all would have been carried on in the machine, or none which would have answered the use that is now served by it. . . . the inference we think is inevitable, that the watch must have had a maker — that there must have existed, at some time and at some place or other, an artificer or artificers who formed it for the purpose which we find it actually to answer, who comprehended its construction and designed its use."

167 Donald Rackin "Blessed Rage: Lewis Carroll and the Modern Quest for Order" in *Alice in Wonderland,* 2nd ed., ed. Donald Gray (New York: W.W. Norton & Company, 1992) , 401.

168 Sir William Empson (1906–1984) was an English literary critic and poet.

169 William Empson *"The Child as Swain"* in *Alice in Wonderland,* 2nd ed., ed. Donald Gray (W. W. Norton & Company, 1992), 348.

the truth to know, Still further inwardly may go... —*Rhyme? And Reason?*

Meaning and purpose in life are found in release from the confines of the purely material world, and a withdrawal of the mind into itself. Carroll, a man divided, very much in this world and, yet, strangely, not quite of it, seemed to be issuing an invitation to share a theological conviction, without ritual or dogma, along with a philosophical dialectic.

PSYCHIC PHENOMENA, THEOSOPHY, AND OCCULT PHILOSOPHY

*I*n the mid-eighteen-hundreds, a gradual transmutation from Neoplatonic idealism toward theosophy and spiritualism took place in England. The cold, barren dogmas of modern science had led to a counter-reaction of mysticism and many Christians had been driven to the beliefs of the Neoplatonic "heretics". Thomas Taylor's[170] interpretations of the ancient doctrines fuelled the interest in theosophy that was growing in England and his influence was evident in references to spiritualism found in Victorian literature and poetry. Carroll was caught up in this wave of interest, making subtle references to it in both his *Alice* and *Sylvie and Bruno* books.

---

170 Thomas Taylor (1758–1835), known as the *English Platonist,* was the first to translate into English the complete works of Plato and Aristotle. He also translated many of the later Platonists as well as some of the remaining fragments of the earliest Greek writings, such as the Orphics, and the Pythagoreans.

Carroll's involvement in psychic phenomena research provides another jumping-off place for exploring his interest in these areas. The *Alice* books abound with, for example, references to thought transference. Alice, standing before the Caterpillar, "thought to herself, 'one side of what?' And the Caterpillar said 'Of the mushroom'—just as if she had asked it aloud." The Caterpillar is portrayed as having perceived Alice's question without the exchange of any tangible symbols. The Caterpillar's perceptual ability was not contingent upon a sense-experience of the ordinary type. He could not have heard Alice's words because she never uttered them aloud. However, he demonstrated an accurate cognition of them. Likewise, when Alice was on the train and the Guard asked about her missing ticket, the other passengers "all thought in chorus" about her dilemma. Alice "heard" their collaborative thoughts as having "said," "Better say nothing at all. Language is worth a thousand pounds a word." Again, no sensory data, in the usual sense, was offered, yet Alice was able to have an accurate perception. In a letter to James Langton Clarke (December 4, 1882), Carroll shares his acceptance of Zöllner's theory, from his book *Transcendental Physics*, of thought-reading being a natural sense, allied to electricity and nerve-force, by which brain could act directly upon brain. Carroll stated, "I think we are close on the day when this shall be classed among the known natural forces, and its laws tabulated, and when the scientific skeptics, who always shut their eyes till the last moment, to any evidence that seems to point beyond materialism, will have to accept it as a proved fact in nature."[171]

---

171 Morton N. Cohen and Roger Lancelyn Green, eds. *The Letters of Lewis Carroll*, vol. 1 (New York: Oxford University Press, 1979), 472.

Perhaps no department of psychical research is viewed with any more scepticism than that which relates to phantasms. Perception may be defined as the cognizance that the mind takes of impressions presented to it through the organs of sense. One class of perceptions are those arising from impressions made by recognizing external, material objects upon the organs of sense, such as sight, hearing, smell, taste or touch. These perceptions are designated as "real" or "true" and are generally seen as contributing to the body of knowledge. However, a second class of perceptions is composed of those that are taken cognizance of by the mind from impressions made upon the organs of sense in other ways and by means other than external objects. In these cases, there is often no evidence that any material object even exists to correspond with the impressions made. Carroll's Cheshire-Cat is an example of these kinds of perceptions. After the Cheshire-Cat made a point of telling Alice that she would see him at the Queen's croquet game, he vanished. Carroll played the concept out a bit further by stating, "Alice was not much surprised by this." Confirming the Cat's immaterial existence, Alice "was still looking at the place where it had been, (when) it suddenly appeared again." After seeing the Cat this second time, "Alice waited a little, half expecting to see it again, but it did not appear." When the Cat finally did reappear, Alice admonished, "I wish you wouldn't keep appearing and vanishing so suddenly: you make one quite giddy." Alice feeling "giddy" as a result of the Cat's rapid materialization and dematerialization, suggests his "real" or "true" existence as an immaterial entity. As further demonstration of the Cat's immaterial properties, Carroll has the Cat honor Alice's request to "stop appearing and vanishing so suddenly" by "vanishing quite slowly, beginning with the end of the tail, and ending with the grin, which remained some time after the rest of it had gone." Here, it has been suggested that Carroll used the Cat's progressive immaterial existence as a vehicle to describe pure mathematics. Although mathematical theorems can often be usefully applied to the structure of the external world, the theorems themselves are abstractions, like a "grin without a cat," that belong to another realm. Carroll takes his theme to fruition at the Queen's croquet game when Alice, fearful of being beheaded, is comforted by the sudden materialization of the Cheshire-Cat. Her first perception of the Cat was as a "curious appearance in the air," which after watching for several minutes she "made... out to be a grin." The phantasm's reality is validated when Alice says, "It's the Cheshire-Cat: now I shall have somebody to talk to." Here Carroll's Cat personifies a perception which is taken cognizance of by the mind from impressions made upon the organs of sense by means other than material, external objects. For, in the case of the Cheshire-Cat, Carroll is very clear that no evidence of any material object exists to correspond with the impressions made. Nonetheless, Alice is able to have sensory knowledge of the phantasm. Carroll, in fact, flaunts Alice's sensory experience of the immaterial object when the Cat makes inquiry into Alice's well-being "as soon as there was mouth enough for it to speak." Alice, in turn, "waited till the eyes appeared, and then nodded." The theme continues as Alice observes that there's "no use speaking to it till its ears have come, or at least one of them." In this particular example, Carroll confines the Cat's materialization to his head, thus accentuating the sense organs of eyes, ears and mouth. After the head had appeared, the Cat "seemed to think that there was enough of it now in sight, and no more of it appeared." Alice's sensory experience with the immaterial object was sufficient evidence to confirm its objective reality.

Carroll's dabbling in psychic phenomena research, theosophy and spiritualism give rise to some other interesting considerations. Upon being published, *"Jabberwocky"* was at once heralded as the best and most original thing in *Through the Looking-Glass*. However, some months after its release, a correspondent to *The Queen* magazine declared that it was actually a plagiarized translation of a German poem. Carroll was adamant that he had no prior knowledge of the poem and that it was his own original work. In fact, he reminded his accusers that the opening and closing stanzas of *"Jabberwocky"* had first appeared in *Mish-Masche*, the last of a series of private little "periodicals" that he had written, hand-illustrated and hand-lettered as a youngster for the amusement of his brothers and sisters.[172] This original appearance was in an issue dated 1855 (Carroll 23) under the heading "Stanza of Anglo-Saxon Poetry," This poem, however, does not demonstrate any mastery of Anglo-Saxon language and poetic tradition. It is inattentive to Anglo-Saxon vocabulary, inflexions and word order. An Anglo-Saxon poet would have used unrhymed qualitative verse, that is, sprung rhythm, as exploited by Gerard Manly Hopkins, and to a limited extent by Coleridge and Swinburne. Although Hopkins was a contemporary of Carroll's, his poetry was not published until 1918, and in Victorian England the experiments of Coleridge and Swinburne in this field were neither fully understood nor appreciated. Carroll's *"Jabberwocky"* was in quantitative verse, with rhyming quatrains throughout. The test of an Anglo-Saxon poet's skill was the extent to which he could vary his words by elaborate metaphors. Carroll, instead, varied his words by portmanteaux, occasionally interspersed with archaisms, and retained the basic structure of Modern English.[173] These facts seem to substantiate Carroll's claim

---

172 Martin Gardner, ed., *The Annotated Alice* (New York: Clarkson N. Potter, Inc., 1960), 191.

173 Anne Clark Amor, *Lewis Carroll: A Biography* (London: Dent Publishing, 1979), 170.

that the poem was his own original work, of which he had written preliminary portions as a youngster.

In reference to the charge of plagiarism, the Dean of Rochester and co-author (with Liddell) of the *Greek Lexicon*, Dr Robert Scott, wrote the following in a letter to Carroll:

> Are we to suppose, after all, that the Saga of *Jabberwocky* is one of the universal heirlooms which the Aryan race at its dispersion carried with it from the great cradle of the family? You really must consult Max Müller about this. It begins to be probable that the *origo originalissima* may be discovered in the Sanskrit and that we shall by and by have a *Iabrivokaveda*. The hero will turn out to be the Sun-God in one of his *Avatars*; and the Tumtum tree the great *Ash Ygdrasil* of the Scandinavian mythology.[174]

Scott's letter makes sarcastic reference to the suggestion that the poem traces its roots to an esoteric ancient cosmology, and reflects something of historical consciousness. He is light-heartedly questioning whether or not it is archetypal and accessible to the person who de-emphasizes external existence, and turns inward. This intimates an occult interpretation of the poem. It is impossible to assess Scott's degree of earnestness about, or motivation for, his comments. However, even with consideration of these variables, Scott's letter provides a strong suggestion that Carroll's theosophical involvements were apparent to selected colleagues. The content of the letter assumes Carroll's knowledge of occult philosophical sources through mention of Aryanism, Vedic references, Sanskrit, and Scandinavian mythology. Many occult systems speak of a Golden Age, associated with an ancient race that lived in the Arctic regions. The myth of the Aryan Race, much embraced by ethnologists and theosophists, was popularized during Carroll's lifetime by H. P.

---

174 Robert Phillips, ed., *Aspects of Alice* (New York: The Vanguard Press, Inc., 1971), 377.

Blavatsky.[175] The main lines of Blavatsky's story of humanity are a reconstruction of a sequence of seven Root-Races on seven continents. She contended that the fifth Root-Race, the "Aryans" was a brown-white race which appeared in Asia. Blavatsky took the Hindu *Puranas,* with accompanying Vedic cosmology, as one of her primary sources.[176] Scott's words "one of the universal heirlooms which the Aryan race at its dispersion carried with it from the great cradle of the family?" reflect the ideology of *Paradise Found.*[177] The Reverend Dr William F. Warren, President of Boston University and member of several learned societies, restated the theory of the Aryan race in *Paradise Found,* by claiming "that the cradle of the human race, the Eden of primitive tradition, was situated at the North Pole, in a country submerged at the time of the Deluge."[178] Warren, especially well versed in German scholarship, tested his hypothesis against the current state of knowledge in the relevant sciences and comparative mythology, and felt that it emerged triumphant. Warren, as a Christian and anti-Darwinian, utterly rejected the image of mankind as having evolved from the ape through a stage of primitive savagery. Warren was credited with having anticipated the later theory put forth by Bal Gangadhar Tilak,[179] the famous pioneer of Indian independence from

---

175 Helena Petrovna Blavatsky (1831-1891). Theosophy is the name Blavatsky gave to the body of knowledge that she developed. It comes from the term "Theosophia" used by the Neoplatonists to mean literally "knowledge of the divine." Her master works were *Isis Unveiled* (1877) and *The Secret Doctrine* (1888).

176 Joscelyn Godwin, *Arktos: The Polar Myth* (Grand Rapids, Michigan: Phanes Press, 1993), 20.

177 William F. Warren, *Paradise Found: The Cradle of the Human Race at the North Pole* (Boston, MA: Houghton Mifflin & Co., 1885).

178 Godwin, *Arktos: The Polar Myth*, 30.

179 Bal Gangadhar Tilak (1856-1920), was an Indian nationalist, social reformer and freedom fighter who was the first popular leader of the

British rule. Scott's comment, "You really must consult Max Müller about this" in reference to the Aryan dispersion, indicates familiarity with the association between Müller and Tilak. In 1897, Tilak was jailed for anti-British writings in *the Kesari,* a newspaper that he edited. Thanks to the influence of Müller, to whom Tilak had dedicated his book *Orion, or Researches into the Antiquity of the Vedas* (1893), the prisoner was able to spend his sentence profitably in study of the Vedas. Tilak's theory contributed to the later development of Zoroastrian H. S. Spencer's book, *The Aryan Ecliptic Cycle* (1965) which received endorsements from dignitaries of the Theosophical Society in Adyar and the Sri Aurobindo Ashram in Pondicherry.[180] Tilak's supporter, Max Müller, founded the series of *Sacred Books of the East* in which he urged British readers to substitute the term "Aryan" in place of "Indo-Germanic", which seemed to exclude French, English and others who, in his estimation, could trace the ultimate root of their language to Sanskrit. The references, in Scott's letter to Carroll, indicate Carroll's awareness of these connections and strengthen an argument for his *Alice* books containing intentionally obscured esoteric philosophy.

It is important to note that this type of thinking had, historically, attracted the attention of mainstream scholarship in Europe. The authors of the *Encyclopedie,* for example, keen to dissent from any Biblical notions that might favour the Middle East as the site of Eden, welcomed an alternative location of humanity's cradle in Asia.[181] Voltaire could not

Indian Independence Movement and is known as "Father of the Indian unrest." Tilak sparked the fire for complete independence in Indian consciousness, and is considered the father of Hindu nationalism as well.

180 Godwin, *Arktos: The Polar Myth,* 35.

181 Leon Poliakov, *The Aryan Myth: A History of Racist and Nationalist Ideas in Europe,* trans. E. Howard (New York: Basic Books, 1971), 183-185.

believe that the preceptors of humanity could have been the rough "Scythians," a catch-all name for the many people inhabiting Central Asia. Voltaire confessed to Jean-Sylvain Bailly[182] that he was convinced everything had come from the banks of the Ganges.[183] The Germans who looked across the Rhine for their *Aufklärung*[184] adopted similar views. Immanuel Kant was attracted by Voltaire's idea of Indian origins.

However, Kant preferred to cite the birthplace of primitive humanity on the higher ground of Tibet. Johann Gottfried von Herder (1744–1803), the court preacher at Goethe's Weimar, placed the cradle of mankind in the primitive mountains of Asia.[185] Herder's Indophilia had a considerable effect on the German Romantics, several of whom became Oriental scholars in their own right. Nostalgia for the East also "made itself felt in two authors who did not much care for India, but admired the Persia of the *Zend-Avesta* and of the Sufi poets: hence Goethe's *West-östlicher Divan* and Nietzsche's *Also sprach Zarathustra*. Further East, it was Buddhism that inspired the philosophy of Arthur Schopenhauer, and, through him, attracted Richard Wagner.[186]

The next question is whether or not Carroll might have even locked cryptic meanings into his texts utilizing something akin

---

182 Jean-Sylvain Bailly (1736-1793) was the founding president of the revolutionary National Assembly of France, when it was first formed in 1789, as well as, at the same time, the first republican mayor of Paris. He was the first organizer of the Paris Guard, later the French National Guard of Gen. Marquis de Lafayette, as well as an astronomer and extraordinary Leibnizian historian of astronomy. Bailly was the first man to be elected a member of both French national academies of science.

183 Godwin, *Arktos: The Polar Myth,* 37.

184 German: 'Enlightenment'; in Germany, the 17th -and 18th-century philosophical movement that emphasized rationalism.

185 Godwin, *Arktos: The Polar Myth,* 37.

186 Ibid., 38.

to the occult practice of *gematria,* providing a different level of interpretation than appears on the surface? In the early seventeenth century, many European academicians subscribed to a system of theosophy which provided keys to the inner meaning of Neoplatonic, Hermetic and Gnostic allegories. This system was expressed in a cryptic language known as *gematria* and for the following two centuries exerted a considerable influence on European thought. The word "gematria" is a late Hebrew noun, probably derived from the Greek *geometria* ('geometry'). It represents a method of allegorical interpretation that, though foreign to modern ways of thinking, was known and used daily by most of the erudite of Europe.[187]

The basis for gematria was the fact that neither Greeks nor Hebrews had numeral symbols other than the letters of their respective alphabets. It evolved that during some remote period of antiquity, when all arithmetical calculation and expression of numbers employed the letters of the alphabet, someone discovered that some numbers made intelligible words. From this primitive discovery it was a short step to spelling words in such a way that the word itself should be an aid to memory, enabling the initiate to recall the mathematical formula corresponding either to the succession of the letters or to their total value.

As fantastic as this may seem to contemporary thinking, precisely this method was employed in such writings as those of Philo Judaeus, Plutarch, and in many Gnostic manuscripts.[188] The formulas concealed in these myths were often numbers that were concerned with geometry.

Geometry, or the measurement of space, was considered to be a science revealing deep cosmological truths. The critical

187 Paul Foster Case, *The True and Invisible Rosicrucian Order* (York Beach, Maine: Samuel Weiser, Inc., 1985), 33.
188 Ibid., *35.*

point, for our purposes, is the fact that from the seventeenth to nineteenth centuries, every member of the inner circle of theosophists who was devoted to the esoteric doctrines was familiar with this ancient system of combining numbers and letters. It is known that Carroll left behind an "alphabet cipher" of his own invention. This was a block grid, or cryptograph, which could be used for creating a coded message by changing any letter in the alphabet into another.[189] Although there is no hard evidence to support this speculation, it is not unthinkable that Carroll, with his passion for creating puzzles, riddles and dilemmas, might have used his own cryptograph when writing the *Alice* and *Sylvie and Bruno* books.

Neither is it unthinkable that Carroll skillfully and subtly embedded other significant symbols into his literature. It is interesting, for example, that Alice noticed that "a large rose-tree stood near the entrance to the garden: the roses growing on it were white, but there were gardeners at it, busily, painting them red." The theosophical trend that was the most fashionable during Carroll's time was heavily influenced by the "meritorious order of the Rosy Cross." Primarily Rosicrucian symbols, as suggested by the name, were the red rose and the cross, or tree, upon which the Old Testament had prophesied the savior would be nailed. Carroll very definitively calls the plant a rose-*tree* rather than a rose-*bush*, "'Would you tell me, please,' said Alice a little timidly, 'why you are painting those roses?'" The gardeners answered, "Why, the fact is, you see, Miss, this here ought to have been a Red rose-tree, and we put a white one in by mistake; and, if the Queen was to find it out, we should all have our heads cut off, you know." In Greek, the noun for cross is σταυρός and, in gematria, its number is the same number as that of ἡ γνῶσις (the wisdom). This would be particularly significant in

---

189 Harold Bloom, ed. *Modern Critical Views: Lewis Carroll* (New York: Chelsea House Publishers, 1987), 77.

connection with the fact that the Greek word for Rose is ῥόδον, and its number is also that of the ἐκκληοία (Church). Rose Cross, therefore, would mean, to the initiated, the "Church of the Gnosis."[190]

"Symbols are keyholes to doors in the walls of space, and through them man peers into Eternity."[191] Throughout arcane theosophical literature, various intoxicating substances have been used to symbolize a power that can take one out of the limitations of one's ordinary consciousness and lift oneself into a higher order of knowing and being. Alice was repeatedly instructed to "Eat me!" or "Drink me!" in order to participate in physical transformations that allowed her to access new experiences. In attempting to enter the garden, Alice "found a little bottle....with the words 'Drink me' beautifully printed on it in large letters." Ingesting the substance reduced her physical size to the point that she was afraid that "it might end... in her going out altogether, like a candle." In order to eliminate this risk, she seized the opportunity to increase her physical size when she "found a very small cake, on which the words 'Eat me' were beautifully marked in currants...." Carroll here uses and same words *eat* and *drink* as in the symbolic eucharistic rites of the pagan mystery schools. This being so, it seems probable that *eat* and *drink* are used here as symbols of spiritual transformation.

"If we consider man as composed of body, soul and spirit, then the Sacred Pilgrim in Greek thought is the human essence engaged in the long and arduous task of finding itself. It is a pilgrim because, exiled from its original state of unawakened spirituality, it is embarked upon a journey that

---

190 Case, *Rosicrucian Order,* 41.
191 Manly P. Hall, *Lectures on Ancient Philosophy: An Introduction to the Study and Application of Rational Procedure.* (Los Angeles: The Hall Publishing Co., 1929), 357.

through the travail of many experiences will bring it back to its ancient seat, but *then* aware of its innate purity and quality."[192]

Ancient historic Greece had two religions, one a public expression which eventually became associated with the Olympian deities; the other, a private expression connected with the Mystery schools such as those of Eleusis, near Athens, and Samothrace, an island off the mainland. In the Lesser Mysteries, the rites and ceremonies presented a dramatic form of wisdom-teaching which explored the nature and destiny of man. In the Greater Mysteries, after more direct instruction, a confrontation was presented between the candidate and his innermost being, revealing a self higher than the daily persona or mask.

Comparison of the rituals of the Lesser Mysteries, as practiced in the ancient world with slight variations of detail, all reveal a universal story of the descent into the underworld. The candidate, egoistically, "dies" in the regions of the underworld, the lower spheres, where he meets and conquers a myriad of difficulties. Shedding his impermanent self, he dies in giving birth to mastery.

In the Greater Mysteries, the passage into the underworld ceases to be a mere ritual. The candidate must now approach "the confines of death" with full knowledge, and in the garment of soul-consciousness pass beyond the veil of order into the theater of chaos. "It is one of the fundamental teachings of occultism that nothing can be *truly known* which is not *experienced, lived through*."[193] The mystic death consists not only in one's ability to receive spiritual light, but

---

192 I. M. Oderberg, "The Sacred Pilgrim in Greek Thought," *Sunrise Magazine,* November 1977, 17.

193 G. de Purucker, *Fundamentals of Esoteric Philosophy* (Pasadena, California: Theosophical University Press, 1932), 258-259.

likewise in one's power to face with equanimity the ravages of entropic chaos. To weld one's consciousness with beings in spheres *lower* than the human is a significant test of the spiritual stamina of the individual. It is, in fact, Persephone's quest.

There is substantial evidence that before experiencing the final soul-shattering vision of the Greater Mysteries, initiates drank κυκεών (*kykeon*), an entheogenic potion made from the *Claviceps purpurea* (ergot) of wheat or barley cultivated on the famous Rarian plain adjacent to Eleusis; or from the ergot of a grass called *Paspalum distichum,* that grows around the Mediterranean. Some researchers[194] postulate that opium might have been an additive to the mushroom-based kykeon. Persephone was associated with poppy and many iconographic motifs of the goddess with poppy pods have been found. Entheogens derived from ergot are principal constituents, in more contemporary times, of LSD. The Eleusian initiates, after drinking the kykeon, then spent the night in a darkened hall, where they beheld a great vision, which was new, astonishing, and inaccessible to rational cognition.

Carl A. P. Ruck, a collaborative researcher, discusses the role played by psychoactive mushrooms in the religious rituals of ancient Greece:

> The ingredients of the Eleusinian potion are given as water, mint, and barley in the Homeric hymn to Demeter, our earliest literary source about the Mystery. Since the mint or blechon (Mentha puliguim) is hardly psychoactive, our attention was directed to the barley. Here our third collaborator, Dr Albert Hoffman, the discoverer of LSD, was able to supply us with the information that ergot or 'rust', a common fungal parasite on grain, contains

194 Michael Ripinsky-Naxon, *The Nature of Shamanism* (Albany: State University of New York Press, 1993) and Christian Ratsche, *The Encyclopedia of Psychoactive Plants* (Rochester, Vermont: Park Street Press, 2005).

a powerful water-soluble drug. Ergot, moreover, like other higher fungi, produces fruiting bodies of the characteristic mushroom shape.[195]

R. Gordon Wasson, working with the Sanskrit tradition of the Rig Veda, has postulated that the original identity of Soma in the homeland of the Indo-Europeans before their migrations into the Indus valley and the plateau of present-day Iran was a particular species of mushroom, Amanita muscaria, sometimes called 'fly-agaric' in English. As would be expected, the Hellenic branch of these same peoples brought with them into the Greek lands a remembrance of a special symbolism for the fungi in religious contexts. Wasson and his colleagues have detected it in the religion of the Eleusian Mysteries, as well as in the rituals of viticulture and its god Dionysus. We should expect, as well, to find this same fungal symbolism in the traditions of the secret Hyperborean offering, especially since that carefully perpetuated ritual, more than any other, preserved a mythical idea of the original Indo-Europeans homeland and its native entheogen.[196]

The Eleusinian Mysteries were the great stronghold in Greece of the doctrine of a future life: and the same doctrine was taught, in definite form, by the Orphic societies which appeared in Italy and Sicily (in some cases close connection with the spread of Pythagoreanism) before the close of the latter half of the sixth century.[197]

Many of the Greek philosophers and scientists were graduates of the Mystery Schools. Notable initiates into the Mysteries include philosophers such as Socrates, Plato, Aristotle, Aristophanes, Cicero, Plutarch and Pindar. The ancient scholars, trained at Eleusis and related centers, were

195 R. Gordon Wasson, Stella Kramrisch, Jonathon Ott and Carl A. P. Ruck, *Persephone's Quest: Entheogens and the Origins of Religion*, (New Haven and London: Yale University Press, 1986), 162-3.
196 Ibid., 251.
197 J. A. Stewart, *The Myths of Plato* (Hertford, England: Stephan Austin and Sons Ltd., 1905), 90.

bound by strong vows to never divulge the essence of the discipline and instruction they had received. So when they wrote, at crucial points in their treatises, they resorted to myth or metaphor, allegory or analogy. When reading the Platonic Dialogues, for example, one would miss the inner meaning if one disregarded the symbolism or veiled hint. In all, therefore, of these types of treatises, who, then, is the Sacred Pilgrim? Is the Sacred Pilgrim a human person journeying through the "cycle of necessity" in a succession of births and rebirths until all of his or her latent human-divine qualities are made manifest? Or is this truly Sanctified One the compassionate entity that enlightened each one of us in the far back night of time when we were not yet self-conscious, when we were still unaware of others, or of space or time? From this perspective, the Sacred Pilgrim is voluntarily exiled from his home as long as he is entombed in material life together with his "child" who does not yet recognize his true nature. The child must traverse the roads and byways of life marked for it by the wheel of rebirth that it keeps turning by its never-ending generation of causal acts and the reaping of their effects.

Metaphorically, Carroll positioned Alice as the Sacred Pilgrim. He cast her, in some sense, as Persephone, goddess of the underworld. Like his literary ancestors, Carroll utilized skillful application of allegory in order to create adventures that paralleled Persephone's quest and pointed to the central theme around which the Eleusian initiations were organized. The symbolism implicit in *Alice* and *Looking-Glass* suggest that Carroll, like so many other writers and artists of his period, used allegory as a delivery mechanism for higher spiritual teachings. Intoxicating substances, throughout arcane literature, for example, constituted a symbol for one being liberated from the limitations of their ordinary consciousness and being lifted into a higher order of knowing and being. Alice's being repeatedly instructed to *eat* or *drink* various intoxicating substances, after having descended into the underworld, was reminiscent of the function of *kykeon* in the Eleusian mystery schools. The *Wonderland* mushroom, suggestive of the *Amanita muscaria,* takes a central position in this context, as the caterpillar instructs Alice to *eat* it in order to change sizes. Interestingly, the caterpillar is a principal symbol for transformation... the foreshadow of the chrysalis. Thus, the symbol for transformation sits atop the transformational agent, the psychoactive mushroom. Further amplifying the suggestion, the caterpillar is portrayed as smoking a hookah, indicating awareness that opium might have been added to the entheogenic mushrooms used in the Eleusian rites. After ingesting a *Wonderland* version of the *kykeon*, Alice's subsequent adventures illustrate the mystic's death, as she summons the power to face, with relative equanimity, every manner of unusual being that the underworld has to offer. Interest in the ancient pagan mystery schools was kindled in Victorian England by the publication, in 1888, of *The Secret Doctrine.*[198] The time was right for the revival of theosophy, with its comprehensive outline of the evolution of worlds and of man. Thus, *The Secret Doctrine* was a principal catalyst that flung open the gates of spiritual inquiry in late nineteenth century England. Not only did it compel analysis of the religious and philosophical dogmas of past centuries, but it also stimulated interest in esoteric spiritual interpretations. Blavatsky's theosophy reintroduced the teachings, largely having—due to the influence of the Church—been suppressed, of the ancient mystery schools. Theosophy, in fact, midwived an expansive occult empire, facilitating cross-pollination with period Rosicrucianism, freemasonry, Hermeticism and Kabbalah, all esoteric, occult

198 Helena Petrovna Blavatsky, *The Secret Doctrine* (London: The Theosophical Society, 1888).

teachings harkening back to the teachings of the ancient mystery schools.

Concomitant with Carroll's interest in theosophy was an interest in the Anglo-Saxon[199] scholarship of his day, as evidenced from his note on Croft Rectory in *The Rectory Umbrella:*

> This rectory has been supposed to have been built in the time of Edward VI, but recent discoveries clearly assign its origin to a much earlier period. A stone has been found in an island formed by the river Tees on which is inscribed the letter 'A', which is justly conjectured to stand for the name of the great King Alfred, in whose reign this house was probably built.[200]

It is reasonable, thus, to suppose that Carroll would have been aware of the existence, in Oxford's nearby Bodleian Library, of the great Junian Codex, containing the so-called Cædmonian poems, adorned with line drawings illustrating the Biblical story. These drawings had already received considerable publicity when Henry Ellis, in 1833, published an engraved facsimile called *The Account of Caedmon's Metrical Paraphrase.*[201] The drawings in the Cædmonian poems are entitled *Anglo-Saxon Attitudes* and depict characters skipping up and down, wriggling and having large hands spread wide apart. When Alice was looking down the road to help the King determine who was coming, she suddenly exclaimed, "'I see

---

199 *Anglo-Saxons* is a collective term usually used to describe the culturally and linguistically similar peoples living in the south and east of Great Britain from around the mid-5th century AD to the Norman conquest of 1066. They are believed to have spoken Germanic languages and are identified by Bede as the descendants of three powerful tribes, Angles, Saxons, and Jutes.

200 Harry Morgan Ayers, *Carroll's Alice* (New York: Columbia University Press, 1932), 67.

201 Ibid., 66.

somebody now! But he's coming very slowly—and what curious attitudes he goes into!' (For the Messenger kept skipping up and down, and wriggling like an eel, as he came along, with his great hands spread out like fans on each side.)" The King assured Alice that his attitudes were not strange at all, since "He's an Anglo-Saxon Messenger—and those are Anglo-Saxon attitudes." Carroll's Messengers appear to have behaviours similar to the "Anglo-Saxon Attitudes" in the Codex material. Further, Tenniel's illustrations of the Messengers, Haigha and Hatta are extremely similar to the line drawings in the original manuscript.

The Anglo-Saxon Messengers in *Through the Looking-Glass*, Hatta and Haigha, are Mad Hatter and March Hare from the Tea-Party in *Wonderland*. Tenniel lets us in on the secret by showing Hatta still with his cup of tea, sandwich and high hat. Professor Harry Morgan Ayers presents some ideas about secondary sources for the names Hatta and Haigha, suggesting that they are simple word changes. The Hare becomes Haigha, which Carroll points out "He pronounced it so as to rhyme with 'mayor,' and the Hatter becomes Hatta.[202] Ayers also reproduces some of the drawings from the Junian Codex in conjunction with Tenniel's illustrations, showing the unquestionable likeness in costumes, body features and attitudes. The evidence strongly suggests that both Carroll and Tenniel were influenced by the Biblical interpretations in the Cædmonian poems while developing both the text and illustrations for *Looking-Glass*. If, as it appears, this is an example of an intentional allusion to an ancient theological manuscript, it further fuels the position that the *Alice* books do, in fact, contain intentional allegorical references.

---

202 Ibid., 66.

Carroll's curiosity in Anglo-Saxon scholarship may, in fact, have been an outgrowth of his esoteric interests. It was the Angle, Saxon, and Jute tribes who invaded Britain in the 5th and 6th centuries and became known as the Anglo-Saxons. Having left their homelands in northern Germany, where Apollo was said to have dwelled during the winter, they were purportedly particularly intrigued by ancient mystery cults. Their ancestral lineage was that of the mythical northern Hyperboreans. The exact location of the Hyperborean homeland was much disputed. As early as 1824, F.G. Welcker[203] had become interested in linking the ancient amber route from the Baltic, where archaeological evidence for Greek contact was beginning to emerge, with certain classical myths, among which he cited as a "Celtic" story related by Apollonius in which Apollo, while among the Hyperboreans, wept amber. In Greek mythology, the Hyperboreans were a mythical people who lived far to the north of Thrace. The land, called Hyperborea ("beyond the Boreas [north wind]"), was perfect, with the Sun shining twenty-four hours a day.

According to Thule Society[204] mythology, Thule was the capital of Hyperborea, supposedly a legendary island in the far Northern regions, originally mentioned by Herodotus from Egyptian sources. In 1679, Olaf Rudbeck equated the Hyperboreans with the survivors of Atlantis, who were first mentioned by Plato, again following Egyptian sources. Supposedly, Hyperborea split into two islands, Thule and Ultima Thule, which were considered to be the center of an advanced, lost civilization whose survivors lingered in subterranean caverns, or according to some legends, within

---

203 Friedrich Gottlieb Welcker (1784–1868), German philologist and archaeologist, was born at Grünberg in the grand duchy of Hesse.
204 The Thule Society (German: *Thule-Gesellschaft*), originally the *Studiengruppe für germanisches Altertum* (Study Group for

the hollow earth. Although the concept of a hollow earth was advanced by Sir Edmund Halley at the end of the seventeenth century, it had actually been introduced earlier by Plato. Plato held, with the writer of the *Axiochus*, that the Earth was a sphere in the center of the Cosmos. The passage in the *Axiochus* is as follows:

> The subterranean dwelling, in which is Pluto's Queen, not less than that of the Hall of Zeus, for the earth keeps the middle part of the Universe, being spherical on its axis. Of this the heavenly Gods have as their portion one hemisphere, and those below, the other—-i.e., the "Palace of Pluto", in addition to its subterranean, or properly "infernal" parts, includes the whole antipodal hemisphere of the Earth, with its sky lighted by the sun, when it is night in our hemisphere.[205]

It was said that surviving remnants of Hyperborea preserved ancient secrets, chief among which was the concept of the Vril, a latent source of magical energy which could be mastered by initiates via magical rituals. Although introduced by Louis Jacolliot, the concept of the Vril was then given new impetus by Baron Edward Bulwer-Lytton, in his work *Vril: The Power of the Coming Race* (1871). Through their mastery of Vril, the Hyperborians, known as the Vril-ya according to Bulwer-Lytton, would emerge from their subterranean sanctuaries and conquer the surface of the earth. Interestingly enough, Friedrich Nietzsche (1844–1900) began his work *Der Antichrist* in 1895 with, "Let us see ourselves for what we are. We are Hyperboreans." With the work of Jacolliot, Bulwer-

Germanic Antiquity), was a German occultist and Völkisch group in Munich, named after a mythical northern country from Greek legend. The Society is notable chiefly as the organization that sponsored the Deutsche Arbeiterpartei, which was later transformed by Adolf Hitler into the Nazi Party. Hitler, however, was never a member of the Thule Society.

205 Stewart, *Myths of Plato,* 129.

Lytton, and Nietzsche in the public arena, the mysticism of theosophy fell on fertile soil. The Thule Society, accordingly, founded in 1918, borrowed ideology from Madame Blavatsky's *Secret Doctrine* (1888), maintaining a history of close contact with Blavatsky's Theosophical Association and followers.

Carl A. P. Ruck, more recently, identified the Hyperboreans as Aryans, and proposed that the Vril was none other than the miraculous *soma,* the entheogenic mushroom from which the kykeon of the ancient mystery schools had been made. So, again, the possibility arises that Carroll, through utilizing the symbolism of the mushroom and Alice's descent into the underworld, was mirroring the lineage of the ancient mysteries. The symbolism of the key and keyhole in *Alice* may, as well, be a reference to ancient mystery practices. Pythagoras, for example, was one of the "veiled" philosophers who revealed his instruction from within a locked chamber behind a curtain.[206] Hence, an esoteric tradition developed that the "keyhole" philosophers or hierophants were the doorkeepers of the *Arcanum arcanorum.* The privilege was only given to a few to take the gold or silver key and open the bolts that held securely the portals of the *domus sancti spiritus.*[207] When Alice first arrived in Wonderland she "came upon a little three-legged table, all made of solid glass: there was nothing on it but a tiny golden key, and Alice's first idea was that this might belong to one of the doors of the hall; but, alas! Either the locks were too large, or the key was too small, but at any rate it would not open any of them. However, on the second time round, she came upon a low curtain she had not noticed before, and behind it was a little door about fifteen inches high: she tried the little golden key in the lock, and to her great delight it fitted!" The theme of the golden key is

206 Hall, *Lectures on Ancient Philosophy,* 327.
207 Ibid., 328.

central to *Alice,* as her adventures all hinge around her desire to gain entrance to the garden. She is either too small to reach the key on the table, or she grows large enough to reach the key but is then too large to fit through the garden door.

In his booklet *The Key to the Understanding of Alchemy* (1924), Rudolf Freiherr von Sebottendorff discusses the history of a Rosicrucian-type Ha ha Yoga, or physiological self-transformation that was introduced to seventeenth century esoterics by *The Chymical Marriage of Christian Rosencreutz* (Johann Valentin Andreae, 1616). Von Sebotten-dorff indicated that the Rosicrucian concept of "Auto-Alchemical Processing," though first formulated in *Charam ed Din* by Sheikh Yachya, probably originated in India with the hermit Ben Chasi, who was a spiritual teacher of Mohammed (570–632).[208] This "autogenous training" is termed *Ilm el Miftach* which means "the science of the key" and those who practice it are called *Beni el Miftach,* or "the sons of the key." Closely related watch-words are, among others, *key* and *rose.*[209]

Many of the esoteric philosophies that became popular in the late nineteenth-century traced back to the ancient mystery schools. According to popular account, it was Orpheus, "the founder of initiations," who had developed the religious mysteries and spiritual teachings of the Greeks. Named after the mythical poet and bard, the sect of Orphism possessed an intensely personal theology that held out the promise of eternal life for the initiate.[210] According to Orphism, the soul,

---

208 Willy Schrodter, *Geheimkunste der Rosenkreuzer* (1954). Translated to English as *A Rosicrucian Notebook* (York Beach, Maine: Samuel Weiser, 1992), 79.

209 Ibid.

210 David Fideler, *Jesus Christ, Sun of God: Ancient Cosmology and Early Christian Symbolism* (Wheaton, Illinois: Quest Books, 1993), 172.

a divine spark of Dionysus, was bound to the body (*soma*) as to a tomb (*sema*) and mankind was in a state of forgetfulness of its true, spiritual nature. The soul was immortal, but descended into the realm of generation until it was released, through certain purifications and rites, to regain its true nature as a divine being.[211] The Orphics participated in the mystical nature of Dionysus in the same way that the Gnostics participated in the mystical body of Christ. Orphism also exerted a considerable influence on Pythagoreanism that, in turn, heavily influenced the Neoplatonists.

Intermingled in Carroll's religio-philosophical inferences are interjections of some serious metaphysical concerns. Alice's identity is in jeopardy when she queries, "I wonder if I've changed in the night? Let me think: *was* I the same when I got up this morning?" She adds, "But if I'm not the same, the next question is 'Who in the world am I?' Ah, *that's* the great puzzle!" The theme is continued as Alice said to the Caterpillar, "I can't explain *myself,* I'm afraid, Sir, because I'm not myself, you see." Likewise, when Alice spoke to the Gryphon, she said, "I could tell you my adventures— beginning from this morning, but it's no use going back to yesterday, because I was a different person then." The essential nature of Alice's reality is targeted as she keeps losing her sense of identity. Although Carroll portrays Alice as continually confused about her personal identity, the Red Queen, conversely, emphatically admonishes her, as she heads into the master chess-game, that it is critical for her to "remember who you are!" It is only in the process of "remembering who she is" and, therefore, being able to make appropriate advances across the giant chess-board that she is able to awaken from the chaos of the dream.

---

211 W. K. C. Guthrie, *Orpheus and Greek Religion.* (New York: W. W. Norton and Company, Inc., 1966), 31.

The metaphysical problem of mortality is introduced when Alice asks the Gnat what the Bread-and-Butter-Fly lives on. "Weak tea with cream in it," answered the Gnat, at which point "a new difficulty came into Alice's head. 'Supposing it couldn't find any?' she suggested." The Gnat matter-of-factly replied, "Then it would die, of course." "'But that must happen very often,' Alice remarked thoughtfully." Pointing up the ultimate destiny of corporal existence, the Gnat replied, "It always happens." The Gnat, in this instance, served as a reminder for the masses of hopeless people who were bereft of assurances of immortality following the nineteenth century attack on biblical revelation.

The question of existence arose from deep within Alice's self and its solution would have to come from the same source — the enlargement of consciousness that would come from the natural outcome of having searched for it. However, there was a painful aspect to this search. The self that was the key to a metaphysical universe was also a function of a physical being and, thus, dependent on physical processes for its development. There was no escaping the physical world nor the mortality that was its consequence. The Bread-and-Butter-Fly lived on weak tea with cream in it until there was no more; then, he died. The metaphysically developed ancients regarded reconciliation with death as an essential element of philosophy. The problem of existence must be reconciled with the fact of one's own mortality. Although Alice changed radically from moment to moment, she was still the same person in a contiguous sense. Alice of the morning might be qualitatively different, in some sense, even seeming dead, from Alice of the afternoon, yet she was the same person because of a continuity across time. Not only did some of her basic values remain over long periods of time, but the self that she was explained and caused the self she became. It was not as if her future self killed off her earlier self. As long as she changed in ways that did not destroy continuity, she could continue to exist, assuring, metaphorically, her immortality, through massive changes in personality, values, interests, goals and abilities. Her immortality, in fact, was directly contingent upon her ability to implement the Socratic imperative to *Know Thyself*.

CARTESIANISM

*O*ne of the portals for Carroll's interest in England's philosophical trends, certainly, was his involvement in mathematics and theology. In a letter to an unidentified agnostic (May 31, 1887), Carroll grapples with the difference between knowledge and belief in his statements about the problems involved in attempting a proof for the premises of Christianity. He borrows the language of mathematics, claiming that some of Christianity's premises are axioms and, therefore, incapable of being proven because proof must rest on something already granted, which is not the case with axioms. If there were anything already granted which could be used in proving them, they would be theorems rather than axioms.[212] Here, Carroll, consciously or not, recites the Cartesian method of pushing philosophical inquiry back to clear and self-evident starting points. Between the 16th and 18th centuries there was a dramatic shift in the way people observed and thought about the universe. This new system of thought was based on the philosophy of René Descartes who promoted a mathematical description of nature and the use of analytic thought—the Cartesian System. Descartes' vision

---

212 Morton N. Cohen and Roger Lancelyn Green, eds. *The Letters of Lewis Carroll*, vol. 2 (New York: Oxford University Press, 1979), 1122.

was to give a precise and complete account of all natural phenomena with absolute mathematical certainty. The method on which Descartes relied for arriving at truth was that of problem-solving in mathematics. The solution to different questions in arithmetic and geometry involved reducing the problem to its simplest essentials until one arrived at propositions which were simple and self-evident enough to serve as reliable principles or starting points from which the answers to more complex problems could be deduced. The Cartesian model indicated that the concerns of arithmetic and geometry with an object were so pure and simple that they need not make assumptions that experience might render uncertain, for they consisted entirely in deducing conclusions from rational arguments. Descartes, then, proposed to extend the methods of mathematics to "all things that come within the scope of human knowledge."[213] He claimed that mathematics provided a universal discipline that would provide the key to a wide range of investigations. As Carroll discovered, while the goals of absolute simplicity and self-evidence may seem appropriate enough when dealing with Euclidean geometry, where even the most complicated figure is constructed of relatively few elements, problems arise when the method is applied to the more complex and varied problems of, for example, religion.

Descartes' early studies in mathematics supported his idea that apparently diverse subjects could be managed in terms of a simple template. A notable success in this area was his *Geometry* (published with the *Discourse* in 1637) in which he demonstrated that the essential relationships characterizing the structure of geometric figures could be expressed algebraically.[214] Congruence between Descartes' position and

---

213 John Cottingham, *The Rationalists* (Oxford, New York: Oxford University Press, 1988), 36.
214 Ibid., 37.

Carroll's *Euclid, Book V, Proved Algebraically* (1874), for example, seems obvious. Carroll, however, recognized that, although the method was sufficient for managing concepts such as shape and/or size, it was not adequate for ordering items such as knowledge, volition, and doubt. The instructions to reduce a problem to its simplest essentials may look plausible enough in dealing with triangles, but what was its applicability to questions about the existence of God or, for example, the soul?

"Pressed by the residual confusions of his education, by the contradictions between different philosophical perspectives, and by the lessening relevance of religious revelation for understanding the empirical world, Descartes set out to discover an irrefutable basis for certain knowledge."[215] Although Descartes' intentions were to refute scepticism and offer a knock-down blow to atheism, the extreme doubt that he employed as a part of his method for reaching truth actually served to fuel the fires of radical scepticism that predominated in the latter half of the seventeenth century. If the epistemologist assumed a doctrine of innate ideas or first causes which included the idea/cause of God, religious premises could withstand a measure of deductive rigor. On the other hand, if the inquirer could not arrive at the existence of God as a self-evident truth, scepticism was a natural adjunct. The *cogito* revealed an essential hierarchy and division in the world. *Res cogitans*—thinking substance, subjective experience, spirit, consciousness, and all of the contents of interiority—was perceived as fundamentally different and separate from *res extensa*—extended substance, the objective world, matter, the physical body, plants and

---

215 Richard Tarnas, *The Passion of the Western Mind* (New York: Ballantine Books, 1991), 276.

animals, stones and stars, the entire physical universe and all of the contents of exteriority.[216]

> Hence, on one side of Descartes' dualism, soul is understood as mind, and human awareness as distinctively that of the thinker. The senses are prone to flux and error, the imagination prey to fantastic distortion, the emotions irrelevant for certain rational comprehension. On the other side of the dualism, and in contrast to the mind, all objects of the external world lack subjective awareness, purpose, or spirit. The physical universe is entirely devoid of human qualities. [217]

The historical progression, from doctrines of innate ideas that intended to provide validation for God's existence, to later positions that were influenced by the advance of science, created problems for theology.

> Paradoxically, the Platonic philosophy had served as the *sine qua non* for a worldview that seemed directly to controvert the Platonic assumptions. All of modern science implicitly based itself upon Plato's fundamental hierarchy of reality, in which a diverse and ever-changing material nature was viewed as being ultimately obedient to certain unifying laws and principles that transcend the phenomena they govern... but those very Platonic assumptions and strategies eventually led to the creation of a paradigm whose thoroughgoing naturalism left little room for the mystical tenor of Platonic metaphysics. The numinosity of the mathematical patterns celebrated by the Pythagorean-Platonic tradition now disappeared, regarded in retrospect as an empirically unverifiable and superfluous appendage to the straightforward scientific understanding of the natural world.[218]

The basis for faith was under examination in Carroll's nineteenth century England and the superficial doctrinal arguments within the Anglican church, as well the esoteric

216 Ibid., 277-278.
217 Ibid., 278.
218 Ibid, 293.

counter-points, were actually symptomatic of this deeper issue. Henry More, centuries earlier, had been an enthusiastic advocate of Descartes until, similarly, his subsequent interest in theosophy caused him to dismiss the Cartesian notion of a material world, consisting of extension, as sharply separated from a spiritual reality. Segments of the *Alice* books suggest, through satirization of Cartesianism, that just as More had grappled with the incongruence between the Cartesian method and his mystical worldview, Carroll dealt with the same tension.

Cartesian doubt came in four successive waves. The first was that our senses sometimes deceive us. Carroll's *Alice* books teem with examples of sensory deception. When Alice was holding the baby that she had taken from the Duchess' kitchen, for example, she noticed that "its eyes were getting extremely small for a baby... ". She looked repeatedly at the baby, while carrying it in her arms, until "this time there could be no mistake about it—it was neither more nor less than a pig... !!" There is no doubt that Alice had perceived her burden as a human baby, for she had grappled with the ethics of taking it away from the Duchess. "If I don't take this child away with me, thought Alice, they're sure to kill it in a day or two. Wouldn't it be murder to leave it behind?" However, in the final analysis, "it was neither more nor less than a pig!!" The same thing happened when Alice, standing in the shop of the Old Sheep, was holding some knitting needles in her hands. "Suddenly the needles turned into oars in her hands, and she found they were in a little boat, gliding along... ". No sooner had Alice sorted this change out when "the oars, and the boat, and the river, had vanished all in a moment, and she was back again in the little dark shop." Alice's senses were prone to flux and error, and her imagination prey to fantastic distortion.

The second wave of Cartesian doubt was that what we think we perceive may actually be a dream. The dream-motif dominated Carroll's writings. Carroll ended *Looking-Glass* with the line, "Life, what is it but a dream?" and began *Sylvie and Bruno* with "Is all our Life, then, but a dream?" At the end of the Trial of the Knaves, it is revealed that all of Alice's *Adventures* had been a dream. In *Looking-Glass* when the noise of the drums had broken up the plum-cake party, Alice's "first thought was that she must have been dreaming, about the Lion and the Unicorn and those queer Anglo-Saxon Messengers. However, there was the great dish still lying at her feet, on which she had tried to cut the plum-cake." However, even the material evidence of the great dish was not sufficient for Alice to conclude that she was definitely not dreaming. "So, I wasn't dreaming, after all… unless—unless we're all part of the same dream!"

The third wave of Cartesian doubt cited that the dream could depict something completely fictitious and unreal. After Alice had related her dream of *Wonderland* to her sister, "Alice got up and ran off, thinking while she ran, as well she might, what a wonderful dream it had been." Her sister, however, sat still "till she too began dreaming.…and the whole place around her became alive with the strange creatures of her little sister's dream." Everything depicted in her dream was completely fictitious and unreal. Carroll points out that if she were to open her eyes, the "lowing of the cattle in the distance would take the place of the Mock Turtle's heavy sobs, the rattling teacups would change to tinkling sheep-bells," "the shriek of the Gryphon… to the confused clamour of the busy farm-yard," and "the Queen's shrill cries to the voice of the shepherd-boy."

The problem of dreams depicting things that are completely fictitious and unreal is different than imagination. Descartes distinguished a faculty that he called imagination from the faculty of understanding, which was the mind's comprehension of truth through ideas.[219] Imagination was the result of combining parts of different particular sense experiences so as to frame a conception of something that would be possible to experience. "A mermaid, in this view, is a creature of imagination, since the conception of a mermaid results from combining parts of two or more particular sense experiences."[220] Further, imagination could combine only a finite number of sense experiences, confined to ones that have been had. Carroll's Gryphon and Mock Turtle would fit the Cartesian criteria for imagination. The Gryphon was, like a mermaid, composed of parts of other creatures. He had the head, claws and wings of an eagle, and the hindquarters of a lion. Likewise, the Mock Turtle was composed of the head, hooves, and tail of a calf, and the shell and front legs of a turtle.

The fourth wave of Cartesian doubt was the condition that if there were an omnipotent God, He could make us err every time we add two plus three. If on the other hand, our existence was not attributable to God, but to some random chain of lesser causes, then it seems even more likely that we would go astray.[221] A Carrollian example of this wave of doubt is offered when Alice attempted to recite, *"How doth the little busy bee"* and "it all came out different." Likewise, when the Caterpillar instructed Alice to repeat *"You are old, Father William"*, she "folded her hands and began," but it came out "wrong from beginning to end." Alice's problems continued when she attempted to recite *"'Tis the voice of the sluggard"* to the Gryphon. Again, even though she had known the verse, she erred and "the words came very queer indeed." Early in her

---

219 Robert Ackerman, *Theories of Knowledge: An Introduction* (New York: McGraw Hill, 1965), 113.

220 Ibid.

221 John Cottingham, *The Rationalists*, 40.

adventures in *Wonderland,* Alice felt unsettled and began to wonder, "if I know all the things I used to know?" In order to test her knowledge she reviewed, "Let me see: four times five is twelve," "four times six is thirteen," "London is the capital of Paris," and "Paris is the capital of Rome." "That's all wrong, I'm certain," said Alice acknowledging the errors. Trying again, Alice crossed her hands on her lap as if she were saying lessons and tried to repeat *"How doth the little... "*. However, "her voice sounded hoarse and strange, and the words did not come the same as they used to do... ". Listening to her own recitation, Alice frustratedly admitted "those are not the right words." It could be said that Alice's errors were either attributable to an omnipotent God who could make her err or to a random chain of lesser causes which would be even more likely to lead her astray.

In Descartes' *Third Meditation*, the meditator inventoried the ideas that he found within himself. One type was innate ideas, which were the ideas that we have of ourselves as thinking things, the idea of God, and our ideas of basic mathematical concepts, such as triangularity. Descartes claimed that the child had within itself all of these ideas. If these innate ideas are, however, self-evident and simply waiting to be discovered, what stops us from discovering them? Descartes' reply was that we are distracted by urgent bodily stimuli that swamp the mind in childhood and by inherited preconceived opinions that obstruct our perception of the truth.[222] Carroll satirizes Descartes by impeding Alice's access to self-evident, innate ideas through the distraction of, for example, constantly changing size. When the Caterpillar asked her to clarify a point, she replied, "I'm afraid I can't put it more clearly... for I can't understand it myself, to begin with; and being so many different sizes in a day is very confusing." Thus, the child's mind was, in Cartesian terms,

---

222 Ibid., 53.

swamped by the urgent bodily stimuli of constantly becoming either smaller or taller. Descartes further stated that inherited preconceived opinions, or obscure and confused judgements, obstruct the perception of truth. The perception of truth was obstructed by obscure and confused judgements throughout the entire fabric of *Wonderland* and *Looking-Glass*. The Pigeon's preconceived opinions about serpents led him to a faulty conclusion about Alice's identity. Likewise, the Duchess' erroneous beliefs about the universality of cats' grins were the result of obscure and confused judgements. The problem of preconceived opinions is epitomized in the Trial of the Knaves when the Queen authoritatively announced, "Sentence first—verdict afterwards." The Queen's logic mandated that the jurors arrive at a conclusion prior to submission of the premises!

Descartes claimed that we can form a clear conception of ourselves as pure thinking things, independent of the body; and that is enough to make body and mind really distinct. This conceivability of a disembodied mind may strike a chord for those familiar with some of the modern defences of a body-mind dualism. Even opponents of dualism are sometimes inclined to concede that it is at least a *logical* possibility that we might exist as pure disembodied spirits. This line of reasoning, of course, is subject to the objection that before we accept a hypothesis as conceivable, we need to ask why conceivability should be straightforwardly self-manifesting? Although this may be obvious in the case of extremely simple and elementary objects and properties, it can lead to problems in cases where we are dealing with something as complex as the nature of a mind. In these cases, that which is conceivable may be a question that cannot be settled by a mere summary judgement.

The waters get further muddied when Descartes states, in *Rules for Direction of the Mind,* Rule III, that adherence to a method of ascertaining knowledge through either deduction or intuition does not prevent one "from believing matters that have been divinely revealed as being more certain than our surest knowledge, since belief in these things, as all faith in obscure matters, is an action not of our intelligence, but of our will." With this admission, the tide turns and Descartes sounds like a first cousin to mysticism. While a young man, Descartes (1596–1650) had attended the Jesuit School at La Flèche and participated in their program of studies that was aimed at reconciling the classical learning of the Renaissance with the scholastic philosophy of the Middle Ages.[213] Descartes' positions on divine revelation were probably influenced by a combination of this early training and his interface with early Rosicrucianism, which came into public notice early in the seventeenth century. The initial Rosicrucian manifesto, *Fama Fraternitatis,* was first issued as a manuscript and circulated in Germany about the year 1610. A second manifesto, *Confessio Fraternitatis,* appeared in 1615 at Frankfurt am Main. Dutch translations of both books came out in 1615.[224] It is important to bear in mind that early Rosicrucianism was not an organized society like Freemasonry, but simply a state of mind. Willy Schrodter, in *Geheimkunste der Rosenkreuzer* (1954) linked Descartes to Rosicrucianism, citing that an initiate called Renatus Cartesius (1596–1650) had identified the "seat of the soul."[225] Descartes had initially become acquainted with alchemical and Hermetic writings from his time at La Flèche

---

223 Robert Maynard Hutchins, ed. *Great Books of the Western World,* vol. 31 (Chicago: University of Chicago Press, 1952), ix.

224 Paul Foster Case, *The True and Invisible Rosicrucian Order* (York Beach, Maine: Samuel Weiser, Inc., 1985), 3.

225 Willy Schrodter, *Geheimkunste der Rosenkreuzer* (1954). Translated to English as *A Rosicrucian Notebook* (York Beach, Maine: Samuel Weiser, 1992), 139.

and his acquaintance with Isaac Beeckman.[226] Descartes' sympathy for Hermeticism was further strengthened by his close contact with the Rosicrucians, and especially the Rosicrucian mathematician Johannes Faulhaber during his time in Germany.

The Rosicrucians were essentially a Hermetic society that sought to understand the hidden order of nature in order to gain power over and through it. Agrippa, for example, wrote in 1655 that "a magician is defined... as one to whom by the grace of God the spirits have given knowledge of the secrets of nature."[227] Hermetic thinkers in this sense divided the world into thinking substance and extension and sought to prepare themselves for the revelation of the hidden truth that lies in "incorporeal substance by banishing the deceptions of the world from one's mind."[228]

Descartes made reference, in the *Praeambula*, to the personal conflict that occult philosophy created for him when he stated, "as actors put on masks in order not to show their blush when cued in the theater, so, as I am about to ascend onto the great stage of this world, having been only a spectator until now, I advance masked."[229] Descartes repeated this

---

226 Isaac Beeckman (1588-1637) was a Dutch philosopher and scientist. Descartes asks Beeckman in a letter of April 29, 1619, to check a reference in a text they had read together written by Cornelius Agrippa, a leading Hermetic.

227 Henricus Cornelius Agrippa, *Henry Cornelius Agrippa: his Fourth Book of Occult Philosophy: Arbetel of Magick,* trans. Robert Turner (London: 1655), 213.

228 Hermes Trismeistus [pseud.] *Mercurii Trismegisti Pymander, de potestate et sapientia Dei,* trans. Marsilio Ficino, ed. Jacques Lefèvre d' Ètaples and Michael Isengrin (Basel: 1532) sig. B4.

229 John R. Cole, *The Olympian Dream and Youthful Rebellion of René Descartes* (Urbana and Chicago: University of Illinois Press, 1992), 25.

claim in somewhat different language in the *Rules*.[230] Why did he believe that concealment was necessary? In part, his concern probably centred around his Rosicrucian connections. He knew already from his time at La Flèche how suspicious orthodox Catholicism was of such Hermeticism. However, he seemed to have hoped that its approach would give him the kind of knowledge he desired. He thus followed this path but knew that he could only do so very discretely. While Descartes pursued this path, also, he was not uncritical of the Rosicrucians. He thought that their efforts were laudable but that they were often lost in confusion, in large measure because they lacked a method for analysing nature and coming to terms with the hidden truths they sought. It is such a method that Descartes believed he could supply. So, Descartes, in many ways, was a man caught in the cross-fire between philosophical rigor and mysticism, between science and spirituality. In this sense, his dilemma was not so unlike that of Carroll, the geometer and the discrete occultist. The principle difference seemed to be in the direction that each of the respective men took toward resolving the tension. While Descartes tended more in the direction of science, Carroll, by all appearance, cultivated more of the mystic's view.

One of Descartes' most renowned illustrations of his method involved a piece of wax whose sensed properties changed over a short period of time. Descartes contended that in spite of change in all of the sensed properties, it was still possible to know something about the wax. Specifically, it was possible to know that it was the same piece of wax at both the beginning and the end of the interval in which it was considered. This could be known in spite of the fact that there were no sensed properties that were retained throughout the whole period of

---

230 He probably derived this notion from Bacon or Pico, as Richard Kennington points out in "Descartes' Olympia", *Social Research* 28, no. 2 (Summer, 1961), 184.

time. Descartes argued that it could truly be said that the wax was the same piece of wax at both times, and that this fact could be explained without appealing to sense experience. What would be known, therefore, in this case, and in other similar cases, could not be fully explained by an appeal to sense experience. However, neither could sense experience be totally discounted in that it may not be possible to form the judgement that a piece of wax was considered without some sensory dependence. Descartes does show, though, that what can be known about the piece of wax was not reducible to descriptions of sense experiences.[231] Carroll's Cheshire-Cat, always challenging Alice's sensory capacities, again attracts our attention. Viewed from a Cartesian standpoint, the Cat is analogous to the piece of wax. What Alice *knew* about the Cat was not reducible to consistent sense-experiences. We are reminded of when Alice was trying to find a way to escape the croquet game and "she noticed a curious appearance in the air." After observing it for a minute or two, "she made it out to be a grin" and *knew* immediately that it was the Cheshire-Cat. Throughout a short period of time in *Wonderland*, the Cheshire-Cat is an entity whose sensed properties change. No consistent sensed properties were retained throughout the whole period of time. When Alice first experienced him, he was "a large cat, which was lying on the hearth and grinning from ear to ear." At their next meeting, the Cat was alternating between appearing and vanishing from a "bough of a tree a few yards off." After the Cat's third visitation to Alice, "it vanished quite slowly, beginning with the end of the tail, and ending with the grin, which remained some time after the rest of it had gone." In subsequent encounters, Alice was able to know the Cat after being presented with only portions, or distortions, of his originally sensed properties. In Cartesian

---

231 Ackerman, *Theories of Knowledge,* 114.

terms, Alice was able *to know* something about the Cat in spite of change in all of his sensed properties.

Another scenario in *Wonderland* that could be interpreted as satirization of Cartesianism is Alice's encounter with the Caterpillar. The Caterpillar, in this interpretation, assumes a Cartesian viewpoint with Alice providing the antithesis.

> The Caterpillar and Alice looked at each other for some time in silence: at last the Caterpillar took the hookah out of its mouth, and addressed her in a languid, sleepy voice.
>
> "Who are *you?*" said the Caterpillar.
>
> This was not an encouraging opening for a conversation. Alice replied, rather shyly, "I—I hardly know, Sir, just at present—at least I know who I *was* when I got up this morning, but I think I must have been changed several times since then."
>
> "What do you mean by that?" said the Caterpillar sternly. "Explain yourself!"
>
> "I ca'n't explain *myself,* I'm afraid, Sir," said Alice, "because I'm not myself, you see."
>
> "I don't see," said the Caterpillar.
>
> "I'm afraid I ca'n't put it more clearly," Alice replied, very politely, "for I ca'n't understand it myself to begin with; and being so many different sizes in a day is very confusing."
>
> "It isn't," said the Caterpillar.
>
> "Well, perhaps you haven't found it so yet," said Alice; "but when you have to turn into a chrysalis—you will some day, you know—and then after that into a butterfly, I should think you'll feel it a little queer, wo'n't you?"
>
> "Not a bit," said the Caterpillar.
>
> "Well, perhaps *your* feelings may be different," said Alice: "all I know is, it would feel very queer to *me.*"
>
> "You!" said the Caterpillar contemptuously. "Who are *you?*"
>
> Which brought them back again to the beginning of the conversation.

In this scenario, Alice is a material entity whose sense properties change over a short period of time. Alice makes this very clear in her statement, "I know who I *was* when I got up this morning, but I think I must have been changed several times since then." The Caterpillar champions Descartes' position that in spite of changes in all of the sensed properties it is still possible for Alice *to know* something about herself. The Caterpillar's succinct statements, "I don't see," "It isn't" and "Not a bit" refuse to admit Alice's assessment that she has undergone so many physical changes that she is no longer the same Alice that she was at the beginning. The Caterpillar stands firm that she could know that she is the same Alice at both the beginning and end of the considered interval in spite of the fact that there are no sensed properties retained throughout the whole period of time. Their conversation opened with the Caterpillar's query, "Who are you?" He was asking Alice about the reality of *herself*.

After being repeatedly unable to answer his question satisfactorily, Alice retorted in frustration by stating that so many physical changes over such a short period of time "would feel very queer to me." The Caterpillar seized upon her reference to the identity of *herself* and countered, "You! Who are you?" which as Carroll so cleverly pointed out, "brought them back again to the beginning of the conversation"!

Sylvie and Bruno

CHAPTER V

The Mysteries behind the Mirror

RELIGION AND PHILOSOPHY

*C*arroll's biographer Anne Clark Amor called the *Sylvie and Bruno* books "Dodgson's personal philosophy."[232] Phyllis Greenacre, in her psychoanalytic study, noted that the *Sylvie and Bruno* books gave the impression "that its author was trying to explain something to himself and to become aware of some inner dilemma of his thought and soul.[233] In *The White Knight* Alexander L. Taylor suggested that the real significance of the *Sylvie and Bruno* books were the way in which they threw light on the creator of the *Alice*

---

232 Anne Clark Amor, *Lewis Carroll, A Biography* (London: Dent, 1979), 194.

233 Phyllis Greenacre, *Swift and Carroll: A Psychoanalytic Study of Two Lives* (New York: International University Press, 1955), 195.

books.[234] These three critics, essentially, all agreed that the *Sylvie and Bruno* books were Lewis Carroll's attempt to put forth a philosophy. Lewis Carroll would probably have agreed with their assessments. In the Preface to *Sylvie and Bruno*, Carroll wrote:

> It (*Sylvie and Bruno*) is written, not for money, and not for fame, but in the hope of supplying, for the children whom I love, some thoughts that may suit those hours of innocent merriment which are the very life of Childhood; and also in the hope of suggesting, to them and to others, some thoughts that may prove, I would fain hope, not wholly out of harmony with the graver cadences of Life.

A key to unlocking many of the mysteries of the *Sylvie and Bruno* books lies in the fairy duet sung by Sylvie and Bruno:

> Say, what is the spell, when her fledglings are cheeping,
> That lures the bird home to her nest?
> Or wakes the tired mother, whose infant is weeping,
> To cuddle and crone it to rest?
>
> What's the magic that charms the glad babe in her arms,
> 'Till it coos with the voice of the dove?
> 'Tis a secret, and so let us whisper it low—
> And the name of the secret is Love!
>
> Say, whence is the voice that, when anger is burning,
> Bids the whirl of the tempest to cease?
> That stirs the vexed soul with an aching—a yearning
> For the brotherly hand-grip of peace?
> Whence the music that fills all our being—that thrills
> Around us, beneath us, and above?
>
> 'Tis a secret: none knows how it comes, how it goes:
> But the name of the secret is Love!

---

234 Alexander L. Taylor, *The White Knight: A Study of C.L. Dodgson (Lewis Carroll)*. Philadelphia: Dufour Editions, 1963.

Say whose is the skill that paints valley and hill,
Like a picture so fair to the sight?
That flecks the green meadow with sunshine and shadow,
Till the little lambs leap with delight?

'Tis a secret untold to hearts cruel and cold,
Though, 'tis sung, by the angels above,
In notes that ring clear for the ears that can hear—
And the name of the secret is Love!

For I think it is Love,
For I feel it is Love,
For I'm sure it is nothing but Love!

This is the quintessence of Carroll's mature religious thinking. His vision of Love as the embodiment of the Spirit of God symbolized the origins and aims of life—strength, hope, faith and peace. In the Preface to *Sylvie and Bruno,* Carroll stated emphatically that "religion should be put before a child as the revelation of love." The *Sylvie and Bruno* books, started in 1867 and not finished until 1893, were dominated by this theme. The first volume criticized ritualism, pointing out that it involved the danger of regarding church services as ends in themselves and forgetting that they were simply means toward the ends of charity and universal love. The second volume instructed the reader in the application of the doctrine of Love. This is indicative of the nineteenth century theosophical intellectual hymn to Love, unique in its theological sophistication and esoteric qualities.[235] The fundamental premise was that "of God's nature in Itself we can and do know one thing only—that it is transcendent Love."[236]

---

235 C. G. Harrison, *The Transcendental Universe.* Introduction by Christopher Bamford (Hudson, New York: Lindisfarne Press, 1993), 14.

236 Ibid., 15.

Carroll carefully introduced his position in a letter to Edith Rix (15 January 1886) when he wrote, "More and more it seems to me (I hope you won't be *very* much shocked at me as an "Ultra Broad" Churchman) that what a person *is* is of more import in God's sight than merely what propositions he affirms or denies."[237]

Carroll emphatically renounced the teaching of eternal punishment and any other scholastic doctrine that contravened the Love of God. In 1895 Carroll completed one chapter of a proposed book on religious problems. The chapter was entitled *Eternal Punishment* and was published after his death by the family biographer, Stuart Dodgson Collingwood. This chapter dealt with the problem of whether the concept of eternal punishment, administered by God, was compatible with a belief in God's infinite goodness and mercy. In 1878 Dr Frederick William Farrar, Dean of Canterbury and author of *Eric, or Little by Little,* had published an anti-damnation treatise called *Eternal Hope.*[238] Although Carroll was taking up an already popular theme, he brought to it something original. His method was to establish a set of propositions that could be handled logically. The propositions that he set out were:

I.) God is perfectly good.
II.) To inflict Eternal Punishment on certain human beings, and in certain circumstances, would be wrong.
III.) God is capable of acting thus.

Carroll examined each proposition for truth. The first proposition he found proven by intuition, facts of spiritual history and answered prayer.[239] In *Eternal Punishment* he

---

237 Stuart Dodgson Collingwood, *Life and Letters of Lewis Carroll* (New York: The Century Co., 1898), 250.
238 Amor, *Biography*, 266.
239 Ibid.

wrote, "This being whom we call 'God' loves us, with a love so wonderful, so beautiful, so immeasurable, so wholly undeserved, so unaccountable on any ground save his own perfect goodness, that we can but abase ourselves to the dust before Him." Proposition III follows naturally from Proposition I and II, for if God has declared his intention of inflicting infinite suffering for sins committed in finite time, he will do so. Since this seems to be unjust, the next step would be to determine whether, in fact, God has declared his intention of inflicting suffering for finite sin. By continuing along this line of reasoning, Carroll eventually constructed an argument against eternal punishment, and in support of a doctrine of Love, with absolute precision.[240]

Carroll touts this theme in *Sylvie and Bruno Concluded* as the characters in the Outland demonstrate a system of rewards and punishments, in no ways eternal, in a transient hereafter. The particular story line that Carroll uses in this case is similar to one devised by Kingsley in *The Water Babies*. As previously mentioned, a copy of Kingsley's *Water Babies* was in Carroll's library, and he had probably read it even prior to publishing his earlier *Alice* books. Although in the *Alice* books Carroll had refrained from appearing in the stories in person as Kingsley did in *The Water Babies*, Carroll appears in the *Sylvie and Bruno* books as the anonymous "I". Carroll's treatment of the theme of rewards and punishments reflects Kingsley's influence when the Professor, by the means of a "Megaloscope", reduces an affectionate and obedient elephant to the size of a mouse that is then sent to Outland with the Empress to live in Imperial luxury. The application of this idea to Prince Uggug confirms Carroll's purpose. Prince Uggug, ugly in both appearance and nature, was deemed "Loveless, loveless!" and, as punishment, turned into a porcupine and confined to a barren cage. "All along the

---

240 Ibid., 268.

gallery, that led to the Prince's apartment, an excited crowd was surging to and fro... against the door of the room three strong men were leaning, vainly trying to shut it—for some great animal inside was constantly bursting it half open, and we had a glimpse... of the head of a furious wild beast, with great fiery eyes and gnashing teeth." When the Professor asked, "What is it?" the answer came back, "Porcupine! Prince Uggug has turned into a Porcupine!" So, just as the loving elephant-mouse had been sent to Outland to be, at least temporarily, rewarded, porcupine-Uggug was sent into the material world to be, for a limited time, punished. To be certain that his point wasn't missed, Carroll had the Emperor summarize Uggug's fate by instructing Sylvie and Bruno: "See the fate of a loveless life?"

While nineteenth century Christianity was experiencing a downward spiral into intellectual narrowness, spiritual arrogance and parochialism, many nineteenth century theosophists were reviving the angelic hierarchies of the early Christian tradition, as taught by Dionysius the Areopagite. In *The Transcendental Universe* (1894), C. G. Harrison details this angelology and unfolds the manifold ways in which the immanent hierarchies of spiritual beings are involved in every level of cosmic and earthly existence. Harrison not only "provides very precise information regarding the 'angels of history,' but also speaks of the nature of evil in a way that shows that the principles of the cosmological vision presented by A. P. Sinnett in *Esoteric Buddhism* and Madame Blavatsky in *The Secret Doctrine* as "Eastern" are actually universal and able to be confirmed by inner experience."[241] There is evidence to suggest that Carroll was, likewise, thinking along these lines. In a letter to Mrs Joan Agnew Severn, John Ruskin's cousin, Carroll advised that he had sent Ruskin a copy of *Sylvie and Bruno*. He

---

241 Harrison, *Transcendental Universe,* 16.

continued by saying that if Ruskin "ever cares to know anything about the book, I should like him to be reminded that he expressed a hope, years ago, that my next book would not be a mere unconnected dream... I have tried to do this in *Sylvie and Bruno*— and that the book contains no dreams, this time: what look like dreams are meant for trances—after the fashion of the Esoteric Buddhists—in which the spirit of the entranced person passes away into an actual Fairyland. Believe me."[242] The connection between 'Esoteric Buddhism' and theosophy in nineteenth century England is clarified in the first sentence of the Introduction to *The Secret Doctrine*, when Madame Blavatsky states, "Since the appearance of Theosophical literature in England, it has become customary to call its teachings 'Esoteric Buddhism'."

The nineteenth century esoteric tradition in England held to a belief in elemental spirits that were analogous to angels. These elemental spirits, although invisible to the eyes of ordinary humans, were interactive with initiates. This is a concept that has pervaded the theological considerations of every era, as can be seen, for example, in a talk given at Esalen Institute (Big Sur, California) in 1968 by Alan Watts:

> We must consider man's relationship with the first of the Nature Kingdoms with which he shares the earth. This one is intangible, non-material and cannot be appreciated by the five physical senses unless they are in a condition of heightened awareness. Its existence cannot be proved to the satisfaction of the scientists nor can the reactions of its inhabitants be demonstrated in the laboratory. Yet, to one with heightened awareness of the physical senses... it is as real as any of the more material kingdoms. The doubter who puts belief in the Kingdom down to imagination or hallucination, will never be convinced of its reality until...

---

242 Morton N. Cohen and Roger Lancelyn Green, eds., *The Letters of Lewis Carroll*, vol. 2 (New York: Oxford University Press, 1979), 776.

scientific research will find the right techniques for demonstrating its existence.

> From my own experience, I know that this Kingdom exists, but other people's experiences do not necessarily convince those who have not had similar ones. Let us define what is meant by the Elemental Kingdom. The ancient and medieval philosophers believed that everything—all matter— was made up of different combinations of what they called the Four Elements: Earth, Air, Fire and Water. They also believed that these... elements were inhabited by beings... which became known as "Elementals." We know this from the ancient myths and legends. Earth, Air, Fire and Water are not elements in the present day meaning of the word, but they are useful and important concepts in esoteric and occult teaching... being part of the angelic hierarchy.[243]

The spirits who inhabited the air were called *Sylphs*. According to old Rosicrucian records, the Sylphs were the nearest neighbours to mankind and were also closest to us in nature. The Rosicrucian novel *Zanoni* (1842), by Lord Edward George Earle Lytton (1803–1873), was a spiritual fiction that centred around one initiate's interactions with a Sylph. An unfinished sketch of *Zanoni* had appeared in *The Monthly Chronicle* in 1838 under the title of *Zicci*. In his letters, Carroll refers to having enjoyed reading *Zanoni*.[244] These elemental spirits, also known as *fairies*, dwelt on the Borderland between the material and astral planes. Carroll's fascination with fairies and elves was not only evident in his *Sylvie and Bruno* books, but also in the early titles, such as *Alice's Hour in Elfland*, which he had considered for his *Alice* books.

Knowing that Carroll enjoyed constructing portmanteau words, with respect to *Sylvie and Bruno*, speculation is ripe

---

243 Alan Watts, "The Elemental Kingdoms," recorded at Big Sur: Esalen Institute Workshop, 1968.
244 Cohen and Green, *Letters,* vol. 1, 214.

regarding the origin of his heroine's name, Sylvie. The "Syl" could have been derived from "Sylph"; the "v" either a phonetic substitute for the "ph" in "sylph", or from "elves"; and the "ie" from "fairies". The little sprite, Sylvie, very definitely dwelt between two planes of reality and interacted with the Narrator. The Narrator, who was only ever identified as "I", demonstrated ability to perceptually participate in a trance state, which could be interpreted as symbolic of an esoteric initiate.

Sylvie and Bruno was designed to make it difficult for the reader to maintain any sort of distance from the material. The reader drifts in and out of Fairyland with the narrator and is, thus, gradually taught to understand that the limits of reality are blurred. Character identity, too, becomes fluid as one person dissolves into another in a series of kaleidoscopic pairings. Lady Muriel is the real world counterpart of the Fairyland's Sylvie, as Arthur is to Bruno. Carroll lets the reader in on this secret when Lady Muriel was talking playfully to Arthur and the narrator interjects, "How exactly like Sylvie taking to Bruno!"

Carroll's choice of the names *Arthur* and *Bruno* also opens the door to speculation. Carroll greatly admired the literary work of his friend, Alfred Tennyson. He read Tennyson extensively and often engaged the poet in conversation about his work. The death of Tennyson's dearest friend, Arthur Hallam, in 1834 dealt a crushing blow to the poet and precipitated his lengthy withdrawal from society. During these years the world heard nothing from him as he kept recluse at Farringford, studying Arthurian traditions and brooding upon the ancient writings of Milton, Homer and Virgil. It was during this retreat that Tennyson began writing *Idylls of the King* (1859), a romantic Arthurian epic which bore the stamp of his grief. At intervals throughout this same period, Tennyson had been composing eulogies on Arthur Hallam entitled *In Memoriam* which not only chronicled his emotions under bereavement, but also made a statement of his philosophical and religious beliefs. The character development of Arthur in the *Sylvie and Bruno* books, which are admittedly a statement of Carroll's philosophical and religious beliefs, is suggestive of Tennyson's influence. A clue to Arthur's identity is found in Carroll's criticisms of the illustrator Harry Furniss' preliminary sketches. Carroll advised Furniss that the initial sketch of the doctor, Arthur, would not do at all. He suggested that, as a model, Furniss use "King Arthur when he first met Guinevere."[245] Another clue is provided when Carroll advised, in the Preface to *Sylvie and Bruno Concluded* that the remark, made by a guest when asking for a dish of fruit at Lady Muriel's farewell party, was one that had actually been made by "'the great Poet-Laureate,' whose loss the whole reading-world has so lately had to deplore." Likewise, after a lengthy discussion with Lady Muriel and Arthur about the "ideas of Right and Wrong", the narrator shared "a view that first made itself clear to me, (as I was) walking out into the fields, repeating to myself that line of Tennyson, *'There seemed no room for sense of wrong.'*"

Much of the thinking central to the British Neoplatonic revival originated with the Renaissance Platonic Academy in Florence. It is possible that Carroll's name choice for *Bruno*, who was the counter-character to Arthur, might have been inspired by the Italian philosopher Giordano Bruno (1548–1600) who, in accordance with Neoplatonism and medieval mysticism, attempted to demonstrate the basic unity of all substances (*De la causa, principio et uno*), and the harmony between the human soul and nature (*De gl'heroici furori*). The influence of Plotinus is evident, via the writings of Nicolas Cusanus, in Bruno's attempt to define human

---

245 Taylor, *White Knight*, 186.

existence as an inner ascent of the soul through higher and higher degrees of knowledge of love. Tennyson praised Giordano Bruno on his deathbed, saying that Bruno's view of God was in some ways the same as his. Bruno, a precursor of the idealistic schools, strove to liberate his mind from classical and ecclesiastical authority, and declared that the emancipation of the will had been accomplished. In *Sylvie and Bruno,* Bruno perpetually questions authority, only recognizing the authority of *love* which binds him to Sylvie. Likewise, Arthur's attempts to ground authority in reason demonstrate that it is founded on divine *love*. Along these same lines, rejection of ritualism was the centrepiece of the first volume of *Sylvie and Bruno.* Carroll's hero, Arthur, the real world counter-part of Fairyland's Bruno, comments that "those 'high' services are fast becoming pure Formalism. More and more the people are beginning to regard them as 'performances'... ". Arthur parrots Giordano Bruno in his instructions to Lady Muriel that one's goal should be to aspire to "the highest motive of all, the desire for likeness to, and union with, the Supreme Good."

Giordano Bruno's position on the emancipation of the will would also have held significance for Carroll. Human will is debated in *Sylvie and Bruno* when Arthur counters Lady Muriel's statement that "... all Nature goes by fixed, regular laws—Science has proved *that* by asking "Is not your mind a part of Nature?" Lady Muriel comes back that it *is*, "but Free-Will comes in there—I can *choose* this or that...." Arthur is relieved to learn that Lady Muriel is, however, "not a Fatalist," which is confirmed by her statement that "Human Free-Will is an exception to the system of fixed Law." This theme resurfaces later in the story when Arthur states, "The causes, acting from within, which make a man's character what it is at any given moment, are his successive acts of volition—that is, his acts of choosing whether he will do this or that." The narrator, "in order to have the point made quite clear," asked, "We are to assume the existence of Free-Will?" The reply came emphatically back, "We *will* assume it!"

Bruno's philosophical system was theocentric. God, for Bruno, was the inner principle of all movement, the one Identity that fills the all and enlightens the universe. He expressed his conviction that everything is contained in this One Principle, "for the Infinite has nothing which is external to Itself." Bruno posited the identity of all souls with the Universal Over-soul. Although he was willing to concede that there were an endless number of individuals, in the end all are in their nature one, and the knowledge of this unity is the goal of all philosophy. Thus, his belief system was essentially theosophical. He admitted his belief in an infinite universe that was the direct effect of infinite, divine power. He defined this power as Spirit, by virtue of which everything lives, moves and has its being. The Divine Presence, he continued, is Spirit, the All-Life, and from It life and soul flow into every thing and every being. Hence Spirit is imperishable, just as matter is indestructible. Thus, Bruno, while accepting the existence of matter, also admitted the possibility of immaterial reality. Bruno's mystical philosophy purported that the ground of all being was a unified transcendental-immanence; the one unchanging spiritual ground of all created things. Carroll, as Pascale Renaud Grosbras has suggested, explored, not only structurally, but also philosophically, a world passing from chaos to cosmos, where cosmos consisted of multiplicity ordered by a *higher*, as opposed to individual, will.[246]

---

246 Pascale Renaud Grosbras, "*La method structurale dans Sylvie et Bruno*"(*The Structural Method in Sylvie and Bruno*), *Lewis Carroll, jeux et enjeux critiques,* edited by Michel Morel (Presses Universitaires de Nancy, 2003).

The potentiality of immaterial phenomena is treated quite matter-of-factly in *Sylvie and Bruno*. The narrator, for example, examining a bouquet of flowers, turned to the nursemaid to ask, "Do these flowers grow wild around here?" when he learned that "the nursemaid had vanished!" Astonished, the narrator queried, "Is this a *dream?*" only to be assured of being awake by "finding Sylvie and Bruno walking, one on either side of me, and clinging to my hands with the ready confidence of childhood." The narrator addressed the question, "But what became of the nursemaid?" to the children. "It are *gone!*" was the reply, to which the Narrator asked, "Then it wasn't solid, like Sylvie and you?" Bruno replied, "No, Oo couldn't *touch* it, oo know. If oo walked *at* it, oo'd go right froo!" In a similar vein, Carroll denies the necessity of sensory experience for validating reality. When Bruno was going to approach a nearby cottage to ask directions to Hunter's farm, Sylvie reminded him that he was not in his material state and, therefore, invisible. "Wait a minute", Sylvie laughed, "I must make you visible first, you know." "And audible too, I suppose?" said the narrator. It is significant that the narrator, the anonymous "I" who was a mouthpiece for Carroll, was involved in normal interaction with the children while they were in their immaterial states. Taking the opposite approach to Alice with the Cheshire-Cat, the narrator did not feel compelled to "wait until the ears had appeared" to speak to Bruno.

Carroll was clear about his own view of the material body in a letter to Edith Rix (25 September 1885): "My conclusion was to give up the literal meaning of the material body altogether." He continued that he accepted "the idea of the material body being the 'dress' of the spiritual—a dress needed for material life."[247]

247 Collingwood, *Life and Letters*, 241.

Carroll's use of the narrator, as the anonymous "I", throughout the *Sylvie and Bruno* books is itself interesting. Just as "Lewis Carroll" became the immaterial counter-self of Charles Lutwidge Dodgson, the anonymous "I" gave Carroll another layer of distance from his corporeal existence. As previously noted, Carroll always vehemently denied that "Charles Lutwidge Dodgson" and "Lewis Carroll" shared the same identity. They were very much two different personae. In many cases, "Lewis Carroll" put forth ideas that "Charles Lutwidge Dodgson" might have been too timid, or too concerned about social reactions, to claim under any other circumstances. As his identity with "Lewis Carroll" had become established with the success of the *Alice* books, he further removed his strong opinions to the province of an anonymous "I". As Charles Lutwidge Dodgson had always denied any association with "Lewis Carroll," so Lewis Carroll denied any association with the opinions of the narrator. In the Preface to *Sylvie and Bruno Concluded,* Carroll states, "I do *not* hold myself responsible for any of the opinions expressed by the characters in my book. They are simply opinions which, it seemed to me, might probably be held by the persons into whose mouths I put them, and which were worth consideration." This claim is shown to be weak by his subsequent qualification, "I have already protested against the assumptions that I am ready to endorse the opinions of characters in my story. But, I admit that I am much in sympathy with Arthur."

In the Preface of *Sylvie and Bruno Concluded*, Carroll also stated that it might interest "some of my Readers to know the *theory* on which this story is constructed. It is an attempt to show what might *possibly* happen, supposing that Fairies really existed; and that they were sometimes visible to us, and we to them; and that they were sometimes able to assume human form: and supposing, also, that human beings might sometimes become conscious of what goes on in the Fairy-world—by actual transference of their immaterial essence, such as we meet with in 'Esoteric Buddhism'." Again, this thematic direction would have been in keeping with the philosophy of Giordano Bruno, a quintessential theosophist, who admittedly believed in sylphs. Like most of the later Romantics, Bruno believed in the supernatural creatures, such as sylphs, naiads, and ondines. Carroll's *Sylvie and Bruno* books hinge on an intricately worked-out series of hypotheses. The first set of hypotheses are that there are, besides the world in which we live, two others. One of these is Outland, a kind of burlesque of the real world; the other, Fairyland. The second set of hypotheses assume that human beings, while invisible and in a trance-like state may observe people and events in Outland; and while in an "eiree" state, may participate in the adventures in Fairyland without losing consciousness of events in the real world. The third group of hypotheses assert that time may stand still or reverse, and that fairies may assume human form.[248]

Carroll, in the Preface to *Sylvie and Bruno Concluded*, specifically outlined the assumptions on which the stories were built:

> I have supposed a Human being to be capable of various psychical states, with varying degrees of consciousness, as follows:
>
> (a) the ordinary state, with no consciousness of the presence of Fairies
>
> (b) the 'eiree state', in which, while conscious of actual surroundings, he is also conscious of the presence of Fairies;
>
> (c) a form of trance, in which, while unconscious of actual surroundings, and apparently asleep, he migrates to other scenes, in the actual world, or in Fairyland, and is conscious of the presence of Fairies.

---

248 Clark Amor, *Biography,* 246.

I have also supposed a Fairy to be capable of migrating from Fairyland into the actual world, and of assuming, at pleasure, a Human form; and also to be capable of various psychical states, viz:

(a) the ordinary state, with no consciousness of the presence of Human beings:

(b) a sort of 'eiree' state, in which he is conscious, if in the actual world, of the presence of actual Human beings; if in Fairyland, of the presence of the immaterial essences of human beings.

In this statement, Carroll's interest in the esoteric trends that existed during his lifetime is highlighted. C. G. Harrison, in a lecture delivered before the Berean Society in 1893, stated that "until quite recently, it was considered a sign of intellectual superiority to rest content with the position of an 'Agnostic' in regard to the most important subjects which can engage the attention of man."[249] However, he continued, "it was inevitable that the pendulum should swing back in the opposite direction, and the reaction from Agnosticism has resulted in a very strange phenomenon—the recrudescence of Gnosticism, a veritable revival of Alexandrian thought in the nineteenth century."[250] He clarified the relationship between nineteenth century theosophy and gnosticism by equating them. "The Theosophical Movement, or the Gnostic Revival, is a very remarkable one, and deserves to be treated seriously."[251] "*Occultism* as a concept dates only from the mid-nineteenth century, as the term for the pursuit of occult science is in deliberate opposition to the prevailing beliefs of scientific materialism.[252] The entire nineteenth century wave of occult philosophy, whether under the banner of theosophy,

---

249 Harrison, *Transcendental Universe,* 67.
250 Ibid., 68.
251 Ibid.
252 Joscelyn Godwin, *The Theosophical Enlightenment,* (Albany: State University of New York Press, 1994), xii.

gnosticism, Neoplatonism or Rosicrucianism was integrally tied up with psychical research into the realm of the super-sensible.

The fundamental premise that governed nineteenth century psychical research was the idea that we might only be using part of our perceptual abilities. The occult philosopher Eliphas Lévi (1810–1875) expressed this theory when he said that there was actually no super-sensible realm, only degrees of perfection of the sense organs.[253] Early psychical researchers were fond of pointing out that many of the lower animals have senses much keener than our own. The object of their research was to explore the possibility of widening the range of human sensitivity to sense data. In nineteenth century occult terminology, an initiate meant one who was able to penetrate the "region of super-physical concepts" which were "hidden by a thin veil from the world of sense, and to distinguish between illusions and realities, which on the Borderland are in close juxtaposition to each other."[254] In the *Sylvie and Bruno* stories, Outland is "on the Borderland." In the Outland, illusion and reality are so difficult to distinguish that it serves as a kind of burlesque of the material world. The three worlds in *Sylvie and Bruno* all revolved around different perceptual standards. In the "real world," sense perception was the norm. Communication was established through speech, sight, sound and tactile experiences. When the narrator met Lady Muriel and her father, he noted that "these were *real* people." When they looked pleased, it meant that they were pleased: and when Lady Muriel said, with a bright smile, 'I'm *very* glad to see you again!' I knew it was *true*." Carroll's access to the Outland, where interactions took place via a garbled, and

253 Willy Schrodter, *Geheimkunste de Rosenkreuzer* (1954). Translated to English as *A Rosicrucian Notebook* (York Beach, Maine: Samuel Weiser, 1992), 84.

254 Harrison, *Transcendental Universe*, 91.

often confused, composite of ordinary sense perception combined with super-sensible perception, was provided through experiencing an "eiree feeling". When the narrator wanted to look at the face of the veiled Lady on the train to Fayfield, he felt that he "—couldn't have a better chance for an experiment in Telepathy! I'll think out her face, and afterwards test the portrait with the original." When no results attended his efforts, he decided to redirect his energies and "think the veil away, and so get a glimpse of the mysterious face—." "Success was partial—and fitful—the veil seemed to vanish… but before I could fully realize the face, all was dark again." When the narrator had, finally, thought the veil away entirely, there was "unmistakably, the sweet face of little Sylvie." Here, Carroll seems to be demonstrating that in Outland the confused composite of ordinary sense perception and super-sensible perception made it impossible to distinguish between reality and illusion. The narrator's next statement, "So, either I've been dreaming about Sylvie, and this is the reality or else I've really been with Sylvie, and this is a dream!" confirms this interpretation. Access to the Fairyland, as opposed to Outland, required participation in the "trance state." Communication was made through telepathy, immaterial objects were real and knowledge was often the result of intuition. When Lady Muriel, for example, invited Sylvie to play the piano, "she seated herself at the instrument and began instantly. Time and expression… were perfect; and her touch was one of such extraordinary lightness that it was at first scarcely possible… " Sylvie's playing had been marvelous, like "the tinkle of the last few drops, shaken from the trees by a passing gust—such that one saw the first glittering rays of the sun, breaking through the clouds." When the parlour guests begged Sylvie to disclose the name of the opera or air that she had played, she confessed that she did not know what either an opera or an air was! The knowledge of the music had come "from within," and was not the product of training or technique. Likewise, when Bruno first arrived in Fairyland, he "ran eagerly to the wall, and picked a fruit that was shaped something like a banana, but had the colour of a strawberry." After having tried to eat it, Bruno exclaimed, "I couldn't feel nuffin in my mouf!" To this exclamation, Sylvie gravely replied, "It was a *Phlizz*" and asked her father, "Are they *all* like that, father?" Here, in the father's reply, Carroll creates an opportunity to point the reader to the reality of immaterial objects, "They are all like that to *you,* darling, because you don't belong to Elfland—yet. But to *me* they are real."[255]

Substantiation of immaterial reality was, of course, a component of theosophical doctrine. In *Isis Unveiled* (1877) Madame Blavatsky claimed the superiority of Eastern and Egyptian wisdom to empirical science. Blavatsky moved to India early in 1879 and took the Five Precepts of Buddhism, known as *Pansil,* during a visit to Ceylon (Sri Lanka) in May 1880.[256] There seems little doubt that Blavatsky, in the tradition of the ancient mystery schools, saw the mission of the theosophical movement as that of offering Eastern wisdom to supplant Western ignorance. The last play written by the immortal Euripedes was titled *The Bacchae.* It was Euripedes' most remarkable drama, composed by the playwright in his old age after he had been sent into exile for exposing too much of the mysteries. In the prologue of the play, Dionysus appears as a god to assert his divine origin after presenting a summary of his travels *in the East.* To speak of his travels in the East marked him as an initiate of the highest secrets of the mysteries. In such initiations, both ancient and contemporary,

---

255 Elfland is "one of the provinces of Fairyland" (*Sylvie and Bruno,* Chapter VI: "The Magic Locket").
256 Godwin, *Theosophical Enlightenment,* 322.

the candidate is always said to have "travelled East."[257] The final chapter of *Sylvie and Bruno*, "Looking Eastward," points to this awareness. As the narrator took leave of Arthur, he quoted the concluding lines of theosophist Robert Browning's poem, "Waring":

> Oh, never star
> Was lost here, but rose afar!
>
> Look East, where whole new thousands are!
> In Vishnu-land, what Avatar?

"'Aye, look Eastward!' Arthur eagerly replied...". 'The West is the fitting tomb for all the sorrow and the sighing, all the errors and the follies of the Past: for all its withered Hopes and all its buried Loves! From the East comes new strength, new ambition, new Hope, new Life, new Love! Look Eastward!'" As the narrator pondered Arthur's words, he mused, "So may it be for him, and me, and all of us!" To which he added:

> All that is evil, and dead, and hopeless, fading with the Night that is past! All that is good, and living, and hopeful, rising with the dawn of Day!
>
> Fading with the Night, the chilly mists, and the noxious vapours, and the heavy shadows, and the wailing gusts, and the owl's melancholy hootings: rising, with the Day, the darting shafts of light, and the wholesome morning breeze, and the warmth of a dawning life, and the mad music of the lark! Look Eastward!
>
> Fading, with the Night, the clouds of ignorance, and the deadly blight of sin, and the silent tears or sorrow: and every rising, higher, higher with the Day, the radiant dawn of knowledge, and the sweet breath or purity, and the throb of a world's ecstasy! Look Eastward!

---

257 Earlyne Chaney, *Lost Secrets of the Mystery Schools* (Upland, CA: Astara, 1992), 182-3.

Fading, with the Night, the memory of a dead love, and the withered leaves of a blighted hope, and the sickly repinings and moody regrets that numb the best energies of the soul: and rising, broadening, rolling upward like a living flood, the manly resolve, and the dauntless will, and the heavenward gaze of faith—the substance of things hoped for, the evidence of things not seen!

Look Eastward! Aye, look Eastward!

Thus the book ends. Just as the final words in *Sylvie and Bruno* are "Look Eastward! Aye, look Eastward!" the final words in *Sylvie and Bruno Concluded,* in answer to Bruno's question 'What makes the sky such a *darling* blue?' are "It is Love." Both books end on the same note from which they began—the vision of love as the embodiment of the Spirit of God. Both books leave the reader with the "theosophist's intellectual hymn to Love": "Of God's nature in Itself we can and do know one thing only—that it is transcendental Love."[258]

SHADES OF ALICE

W hen Carroll set out to write the *Sylvie and Bruno* books, he was firmly resolved that the project should be completely different than the *Alice* books.

Anything that would have the effect of connecting the book with *Alice* would be absolutely disastrous, he wrote. The thing I wish above all to avoid in this new book is the giving of any pretext for critics to say 'this writer can only play one tune: the book is a rechauffe of *Alice*.' I'm trying my very best to get out of the old groove, and to have no 'connecting link' whatever.[259]

258 Harrison, *Transcendental Universe,* 15.
259 Anne Clark Amor, *Lewis Carroll, A Biography* (London: Dent, 1979), 246.

Although Carroll's intentions were, as stated, to create a completely fresh work with *Sylvie and Bruno*, he replayed enough thematic material from the *Alice* books to make it hard to accept his claim at face value. These replays begin with obvious superficial similarities in the acrostic poems of the names of child-friends and move on to more significant themes. Just as, for example, *Through the Looking-Glass* ends with an acrostic poem of Alice Pleasance Liddell's name, *Sylvie and Bruno* begins with an acrostic of child-friend Isa Bowman's name. More significantly, both of these poems provide windows into Carroll's mystical perspective. In some sense, "this writer *could* only play one tune": his vision of Love as the embodiment of the Spirit of God, for this was at the forefront of his consciousness. Through radical deconstruction of a purely material worldview, Carroll cultivates the conditions, in both works, for an esoteric interpretation of reality.[260] The poem in *Looking-Glass* ends:

> Ever drifting down the stream—
> Lingering in the golden gleam—
> Life, what is it but a dream?

The poem in *Sylvie and Bruno* begins:

> Is all our Life, then, but a dream
> Seen faintly in the golden gleam
> Athwart Time's dark resistless stream?

Sylvie and Bruno shares further congruence with *Alice* through parallel treatments of time, space and gravity.[261] Just as Alice's experiences in Wonderland included a series of

---

260 See Chapters I: *Myths Behind the Maker* and V: *Platonism, Neoplatonism and Gnosticism*.

261 See *Time, Space, and Gravity* in Chapter IV above.

changes in her physical size, so did Sylvie and Bruno's experiences in Fairyland:

> 'We must go back into the wood now,' Sylvie said, as soon as we were out of hearing. 'We can't stay this size any longer.' 'Then you will be quite tiny Fairies, again, next time we meet?' 'Yes,' said Sylvie.

To the narrator's worried questioning about the Outlandish Watch being too large for the children to carry when they resumed their fairy-size, Bruno replied, "When we go small, it'll go small!" Just as it had been necessary for Alice to get smaller to gain access to the garden, Sylvie and Bruno, likewise, "must go small when the sun sets" in order to return to Fairyland.

Carroll's lifelong interest in the question 'When does the day begin?'[262] is, as well, only thinly disguised in the *Sylvie and Bruno* books. In a manner similar to the *Alice* books, the nature of perception is explored as Arthur, at the Farewell Party, questions "when he began to own his soup." "Up to the moment of its being put into the plate, it was the property of our host: while being offered round the table, it was, let us say, held in trust by the waiter: did it become mine when I accepted it? Or when it was placed before me? Or when I took the first spoonful? This theme, addressed repeatedly in the *Alice* books, resurfaces in *Sylvie and Bruno* as Carroll, potentially referencing Berkeley, presents an argument from perceptual relativity.[263] Although originating with the Greek skeptics, this argument had been reformulated, by the ardent seventeenth century French Platonist Simon Foucher, as a tool for critiquing Cartesianism.

---

262 See *Time, Space, and Gravity* in Chapter IV above.
263 See Berkeley, *Dialogues* 142-3 [722-23] for the argument from perceptual relativity.

Variations on this same argument extend into the relative perception of temporality. Time themes surface in the *Sylvie and Bruno* books, as they did in *Alice,* when disturbances in time are dominated by condensation of past and present. As the Earl and Arthur speculate on a house, "placed a few billion miles above a planet" falling to the planet, Lady Muriel queries, "And is five-o'clock tea to be going on all the while?" Past and present are condensed into a perpetual "five o'clock." The theme is repeated when Mein Herr explains how some people "store up the useless hours: and, on some *other* occasion, when they happen to *need* extra time, ... get them out again."

As he had done in the *Alice* books, Carroll explores the distinction between "time" and the "o'clock," as absolute and relative aspects of temporality, in *Sylvie and Bruno* with his tale of the "Professor's Outlandish Watch." The Outlandish Watch "has the peculiar property that, instead of *its* going with the *time,* the *time* goes with *it.*" Here Carroll is playing out the same theme as he had in The Mad Tea-Party, but he has reversed the circumstances. Whereas the Mad Hatter had claimed that "if you kept on good terms with Time, he'd do almost anything you liked with the clock," the Professor's Outlandish Watch made Carroll's point by reversing the process—the clock could do almost anything with time! The "o'clock" of the Outlandish Watch had no real relevance to a conception of absolute Time. Instead, time, in the quantitative sense, was merely the invention of the clock. The Hatter's remark, if it were "nine o'clock in the morning, just time to begin lessons: you'd only have to whisper a hint to Time, and round goes the clock in a twinkling! Half-past one, time for dinner!" is essentially the same as the Professor's statement that, "if I move the hands, I change the time." The Professor amplifies that claim by adding, "I can move them as much as a month *backwards...* and then you have the events all over again." Carroll's point, in fact, is best summed up by the Professor's explanation that as long as the Outlandish Watch is "let alone, it takes its own course. Time has no effect on it."

In *Sylvie and Bruno* the Outlandish Watch had a "Reversal Peg" that made "the events of the next hour happen in the reverse order." Carroll had created the same scenario in *Looking-Glass* when Alice spied the Red Queen, fond of "living backwards," a long way off and decided to get to her "by walking in the opposite direction." Alice's plan had "succeeded beautifully." When the narrator of *Sylvie and Bruno* pushed the Reversal Peg on the Outlandish Watch, everything took place backwards. In dining, for example, "an empty fork is raised to the lips: there it receives a neatly-cut piece of mutton, and swiftly conveys to the plate, where it instantly attaches itself to the mutton already there." This scenario is strikingly similar to Alice, in *Looking-Glass,* "handing the cake around first, and cutting it afterwards." As Alice carried the cake around, it divided itself into three pieces. "'*Now* cut it up,' said the Lion, as she returned her plate with the empty dish." All of these scenarios are playfully suggestive of Plato's conception of Time, as presented in the *Statesman*:

> Str. Listen, then. There is a time when God himself guides and helps to roll the world in its course; and there is a time, on the completion of a certain cycle, when he lets go, and the world being a living creature, and having originally received intelligence from its author and creator turns about and by an inherent necessity revolves in the opposite direction.
> Y. Soc. Why is that?
> Str. Why, because only the most divine things of all remain ever unchanged and the same, and body is not included in this class. Heaven and the universe, as we have termed them, although they have been endowed by the Creator with many glories, partake of a bodily nature, and therefore cannot be entirely free from perturbation. But their motion is, as far as possible, single and in the same place, and of the same kind; and is therefore only subject

to a reversal, which is the least alteration possible. For the lord of all moving things is alone able to move of himself; and to think that he moves them at one time in one direction and at another time in another is blasphemy. Hence we must not say that the world is either self-moved always, or all made to go round by God in two opposite courses; or that two Gods, having opposite purposes, make it move round. But as I have already said (and this is the only remaining alternative) the world is guided at one time by an external power which is divine and receives fresh life and immortality from the renewing hand of the Creator, and again, when let go, moves spontaneously, being set free at such a time as to have, during infinite cycles of years, a reverse movement: this is due to its perfect balance, to its vast size, and to the fact that it turns on the smallest pivot.

Plato posited that time was created when the creator fashioned the world from existing material, giving form to primitive matter. Plato, further, in the *Timaeus* argued that the creator

sought to make the universe eternal, so far as might be. Now the nature of the ideal being was everlasting, but to bestow this attribute in its fullness upon a creature was impossible. Wherefore he resolved to have a moving image of eternity, and when he set in order the heavens, he made this image eternal but moving, according to number, while eternity itself rests upon unity; and this image we call Time.

According to Plato then, time was created at the same instant as the heavens. Viewing time as a moving image of eternity, all of humanity stands poised between the present moment and the timeless immensity of the eternal. St. Augustine, in agreeing that time began with the creation, was responsible for bringing much of Plato's perspective into Christianity. This interpretation of time persisted until the work of Galileo and Newton revisioned time as an independent entity with its own quantitative value. The universe no longer determined time, as Newton postulated an absolute clock, external to the universe, which measured time independently of the universe itself. This concept repositioned time in quantitative mathematics, relating motion, through Newton's theory of fluxions, to the universal flux of time. No longer could time be considered an illusion as the ancient philosophers had suggested, for now the whole of science was being built on laws based totally on the notion of mechanical time. As demonstrated in Chapter IV, Carroll's apparent intrigue with the concept of time from a psycho-spiritual viewpoint could not be reconciled with his distrust of the implications of the application of quaternions to geometry nor the resultant concept of a curved space-time, predicated on principles of non-Euclidean geometry. The concept of time, therefore, left Carroll grappling with an obvious, and serious, philosophical conundrum that we see him, consciously or not, dealing with in both the *Alice* and *Sylvie and Bruno* books.

The concept of gravity, similarly, receives attention in the *Sylvie and Bruno* books, as it had in *Alice*. Mein Herr tells Lady Muriel that in his country "they run their railway-trains without any engines—nothing is needed but machinery to *stop* them." Asked "where does the *force* come from," Mein Herr replied "they use the force of *gravity*. It is a force known also in *your* country, I believe?" The Earl remarked that, "but that would need a railway going *down-hill*... you can't have all your railways going down-hill?" "They *all* do... from *both* ends," answered Mein Herr. Carroll further parodies the issue of gravity in Mein Herr's explanation of the technique. "Each railway is in a long tunnel, perfectly straight: so of course the *middle* of it is nearer the center of the globe than the two ends: so every train runs half-way *down*-hill, and that gives it force enough to run the *other* half *up* hill."

Principles of relative interpretation are suggested regarding the laws of falling bodies when Arthur claims that "one can easily imagine a situation where things would *necessarily* have no weight, relative to each other, though each would have its usual weight, looked at by itself." He amplified his position by saying that "nothing can be *heavy*... except by *trying* to fall, and being prevented from doing so." He continued:

> Well, now, if I take this book, and hold it out at arm's length, of course, I feel its *weight*. It is trying to fall, and I prevent it. And, if I let go, it falls to the floor. But, if we were all falling together, it couldn't be *trying* to fall any quicker, you know; for, if I let go, what more could it do than fall? And, as my hand would be falling, too—at the same rate—it would never leave it, for that would be to get ahead of it in the race. And it could never overtake the falling floor!

Thus, despite Carroll's stated intentions of keeping *Sylvie and Bruno* completely distinct from the *Alice* books, the similarities are too obvious to miss. Certain critical, philosophical themes are recycled as Carroll, obviously, could not abandon them. We are reminded of Alice's conversation with the Caterpillar in Wonderland when the Gardener, in *Sylvie and Bruno* asks Sylvie who Bruno is. When Sylvie replied, "He's my brother," the Gardener anxiously queried, "Was he your brother yesterday?" After being assured that he was, the Gardener explained the source of his concern by stating that "Things do change so, here. Whenever I look again it's sure to be something different!"

Sylvie and Bruno's struggle to get through a door in the garden-wall is, likewise, a familiar theme. "The Gardener... produced a handful of keys—one large one, and a number of small ones... and patiently tried all the small keys, over and over again." This emphasis on the key[264] continues as the Professor suggested, "Why not try the *large* one? I have often

---

264 See *Psychic Phenomena, Theosophy, and Occult Philosophy* in Chapter IV above.

observed that a door unlocks *much* more nicely with its *own* key." "The very first trial of the large key proved a success: the Gardener opened the door... " After having let Sylvie, Bruno and the Professor through the door, the Gardener re-locked the door behind them, singing, "He thought he saw a Garden-Door that opened with a key...." " Therefore, just as the key, a symbol of initiation, had played a critical role in Alice's access to the super-sensible experiences in Wonderland, so did it factor into Sylvie and Bruno's ability to return to Fairyland.

While Alice's entrance into Wonderland had required a descent "down, down, down" into the earth, Sylvie and Bruno's travel to Fairyland involved sinking into the earth. The children were instructed to follow an old man in ragged dress as he waved his hands over a bush "which began instantly to sink into the earth." The narrator recounts that "when the bush had sunk quite out of our sight, marble steps were seen, leading downwards into darkness. The old man led the way, and we eagerly followed. The staircase was so dark, at first, that I could only just see the forms of the children, as, hand-in-hand, they groped their way down after their guide: but it got lighter every moment, with a strange silvery brightness, that seemed to exist in the air, as there were no lamps visible; and, when at last we reached a level floor, the room we found ourselves in was almost as light as day." Sylvie and Bruno learned that they were in Elfland, a province of Fairyland and that they had descended one thousand miles into the earth. This theme seemed to hold particular significance for Carroll. In both sets of books Carroll appears to allegorize ancient mythology, re-popularized during his lifetime by the influence of theosophy. Plato's history of the soul, for example, drew heavily upon the Pythagorean Orphics, who put purification in the forefront of their eschatology. The eschatology of the Pythagorean Orphics may be broadly categorized as celestial and astronomical. The Soul falls from its native place in the Highest Heaven, through the Heavenly Spheres, to its first incarnation on Earth. By means of a series of sojourns in Hades, and re-incarnations on Earth, it is purified from the taint of the flesh.[265] The source for this eschatology, if the carefully formed view of Albrecht Dieterich is accepted, was a popular Orphic Manual, the *Descent to Hades*, in which the vicissitudes endured by the immortal Soul were described.[266] Pythagoras, an hierophant of Great Mother mysteries with an Anatolian stamp, offered Platonism a new doctrine, probably influenced by Indo-Iranian sources, of immortality.[267] The purest form of inquiry was mathematical. Here one is freed from reliance on the senses and can proceed immaterially, deducing results from self-evident truths. The uncertainties of the empirical realm are transcended.[268] Mathematics was, thus, an agent to release the soul from its close tie to the body and, as such, become a principal agent of purification. While Pythagoreanism remained closely related to Orphic thought of the period, the clearly distinguishing factor between the two was that for the Pythagoreans liberation was not obtained through religious rite, but through philosophy, the contemplation of first principles. Hence, *philosophia* was a form of purification, a way to immortality.[269] This influence is clearly seen in Plato's *Phaedo*, where symbolic death represents the goal of all true philosophy, so that pure truth may be apprehended by the

---

265 Walter Burkett, *Lore and Science in Ancient Pythagoreanism.* Translated by Edwin L. Minar, Jr. (Cambridge, MA: Harvard University Press, 1972), 313.

266 J. A. Stewart, *The Myths of Plato* (Hertford, England: Stephan Austin and Sons Ltd., 1905), 91.

267 Burkett, *Ancient Pythagoreanism,* 165.

268 Roy Sorensen, *A Brief History of the Paradox* (Oxford: Oxford University Press, 2003), 22.

269 Kenneth Sylvan Guthrie, *The Pythagorean Sourcebook and Library* (Grand Rapids, Michigan: Phanes Press, 1987), 31.

soul, in its pure state.[270] The parallel is close between Plato's geography of Tartarus and the True Surface of the Earth, and Dante's geography of Hell and the Mount of Purgatory with the Earthly Paradise on its summit.[271] The *Phaedo* and the *Divina Commedia* make Tartarus or Hell a chasm bored right through the globe of the Earth with two antipodal placed openings.[272] Tartarus is the lowest region of the world, as far below earth as earth is from heaven. While Hades is the main realm of the dead in Greek mythology, Tartarus also contained a number of characters. In early stories, it is primarily the prison for defeated gods. However, in later myths Tartarus became a place of punishment for sinners. It resembled Hell and was the opposite of Elysium, the afterlife for the blessed. In ancient Orphic sources, and in the mystery schools, however, Tartarus was the unbounded first cause from which the Light and the cosmos were born.

Plato's myth taught that the earth was spherical, in the middle of the heavens, and in perfect equilibrium. This earth was, further, incredibly vast, and the known world was but one of many hollow places in the earth where water and mist and air gathered. The true surface of the earth, far above us, was a pure ether and we were like creatures living at the bottom of the sea who assumed they were on the surface of the earth... and that the sea was the sky. The hollow regions of the earth were connected by great subterranean rivers of water, fire, and mud that flowed between the several regions. One of the cavities in the earth was so large and so deep that it pierced right through to the other side of the earth. This cavity, referred to as Tartarus, was where all of the rivers flowed together. When people died, those who lived a neutral life spent certain periods of time in the underworld, where they

---

270 Ibid., 211.
271 Stewart, *Myths of Plato* , 119-120.
272 *Phaedo*, 111E; *Inferno*, xxxiv., *sub fin.*

were punished for their sins and rewarded for their good deeds, and were then returned to the earth once more. Those who had completely purified themselves through philosophy lived without a body altogether, and would reach places indescribably more beautiful even than the true surface of the earth.

Obviously, Plato's myth is not intended as a literal account of the earth or the afterlife. The critical thrust of the myth lies in the contrast between the world as we know it and the true surface of the earth. The analogy here is to the contrast between the sensible, immanent world and the invisible, transcendent world of Forms. Just as what we see and touch are pale reflections of the Forms in which sensible objects participate, the world we inhabit is a pale reflection of the true surface of the earth.

According to the myth, people who lived on the true surface of the earth could speak directly with the gods and see the sun and moon as they truly were. By contrast, the ancient Greeks could only communicate with their gods through oracles, and a proper understanding of the heavens was considered the highest and most difficult task of physics. The people who lived on the true surface of the earth were the model philosophers who, through an understanding of the Forms, could see things for what they really were.

Plato's myth, and his account of the afterlife, had a profound effect on Christianity. Plato's account is an early version of the Christian ideal, in which our fate after death is determined by our virtue in this life. The significant difference was that the good for Plato are not those who possess Christian virtues, but those who possess a knowledge of The Forms. This approach posited that, by starting with foundational basic principles, like the axioms of geometry, the rest of all possible knowledge could deductively be derived, including a direct experience of Ultimate Reality. Thus, we find an appeal to a type of spiritual rationalism or an *a priori* spirituality.

Just as symbolic death represents the goal of all true philosophy, the death of the ego is the goal of mysticism. As long as the ego dominates, there is no room for Love to be the operative modality. The Dark Night of the Soul, occurring like an initiation before one is admitted into regular relationship with higher consciousness, signifies the loosening of the ego's grip. The Dark Night of the Soul required a descent "down, down, down" into "the earth," into the dark and shadowy elements of the soul. For, the depths of the soul contained those unbounded first causes from which the Light of spirituality was born. Plato's history of the soul mapped out the initiatory descent of the mystic. The adventures of Alice, "down, down, down" the rabbit-hole, foreshadow Sylvie and Bruno's travel to Fairyland where, symbolically, Carroll offers the reader an allegory for the death of the ego, making room for the in-dwelling of Love.

More superficially, the *Sylvie and Bruno* books also offer instances where word plays and incidental exchanges seem like re-enactments of *Alice*. These superficialities come across like window dressing, intended to start the reader on a treasure hunt for Carroll's deeper philosophical themes. One is reminded of the Duchess telling Alice that "everything's got a moral, if only you can find it" when the narrator asked Sylvie if "Bruno's story will have a Moral to it?" "'I *think* so,' Sylvie replied doubtfully. 'There generally *is* a Moral, only he puts it in too soon.'" Likewise, when the wife of Outland's Warden intended to "growl", "though it was more like... purring", it is reminiscent of the scene in *Wonderland* where the Cheshire-Cat calls his "purr" a "growl". As typical in some of the other aforementioned instances, a single theme is simply re-worked in reverse. Whereas the Cheshire-Cat's "purr" is called a "growl", the Warden's wife's "growl" is called a "purr". Again, when "Bruno was at the window, trying to throw out his slice of plum-cake" to an old Beggar, it builds on the Knight's suggestion to Alice that they had better take a plate with them as "it would come in handy if we find any plum-cake."

The Pigeon's conclusion, in *Wonderland,* that "little girls were a kind of serpent" because they ate eggs points to resemblance theory. Platonism, and particularly Neo-platonism, dispensed with substantive universals, by claiming that what unites a group of objects of the same kind is that they resemble one of their number taken as a standard. This principle expressed the motivation underlying Plato's Theory of the Forms. Where there are a number of objects of the same kind, or sharing a single property, it is deemed apparent that there must be a single something which is this kind or property, and which therefore gets treated as an abstract non-material substance. In a strict sense, this principle could be seen as simply giving a motive for postulating universals. In *Sylvie and Bruno,* the same concept is developed when the Professor could not tell the Gardener from the Lion. "'But you must explain to me, please,' the Professor said with an anxious look, '*which* is the Lion, and *which* is the Gardener. It's *most* important not to get two such animals confused together. And one's very likely to do it in their case—-both having mouths, you know.'" When Bruno asked the Professor if he always confused things of this type, he replied, "Pretty often, I'm afraid... for instance there's the rabbit-hutch and the hall-clock. One gets a little confused with *them*—both having doors, you know."

Carroll's plan of using the *Sylvie and Bruno* books "of suggesting... some thoughts that may prove... not wholly out of harmony with the graver cadences of Life" gives the books a vaguely instructional air. More of the presumption of the tales being merely "children's stories" is lost as direct references are made to the prevailing intellectual influences of the day. For example, Darwin is ridiculed when a conversation on the train turns to the benefits of steam engines. A lady remarked, "But the booklets—the little thrilling romances, where the Murder comes at page fifteen, and the Wedding at page forty—surely *they* are due to Steam?" The narrator replied, "And when we travel by Electricity—if I may venture to develop your theory—we shall have leaflets instead of booklets, and the Murder and the Wedding will come on the same page." "'A development worthy of Darwin!' the lady exclaimed enthusiastically." Additionally, the virtues of Shelley, Browning, Tennyson, and Shakespeare are extolled through individual mention. Haydn's symphonies are referred to as "heavenly modulations." Paley's definition of *virtue* is condemned as "utterly selfish." At one point Arthur, engaged in conversation with "the metaphysical young lady" at Lady Muriel's party, made an "ingenious jumble... of Spencer's words":

> "Talking to Herbert Spencer," he began, "do you really find no logical difficulty in regarding Nature as a process of involution, passing from definite coherent homogeneity to indefinite heterogeneity?"

Albeit amusing, this is neither language nor conceptualization that is geared to children. "The graver cadences of Life" are, more accurately, both directly and indirectly targeted to Carroll's Victorian peers. The mystic's concern with the nature of reality and the distinction between absolute and relative experience, as demonstrated through Carroll's preoccupation with issues of size, time and gravity, is of foremost consideration. Playing on the idea of reversals, as well, Carroll explores the transitory nature of various forces, otherwise considered sacrosanct. Finally, and most importantly, esoteric interest in ancient initiatory themes are found throughout Carroll's work. He tells the story, in veiled terms, of mystery schools and gnosis.

In sum, far from being merely children's literature, the *Sylvie and Bruno* books accompany *Alice* by representing an allegorical statement of Carroll's quest for the purpose of life, as alluded to in the Preface:

> But, once realize what the true object *is* in life—that it is *not* pleasure, *not* knowledge, *not* even fame itself, "that last infirmity of noble minds"—but that it *is* the development of *character,* the rising to a higher, nobler, purer standard, the building-up of the perfect Man—and then, so long as we feel that this is going on, and will (we trust) go on for evermore, death has for us no terror; it is not a shadow, but a light; not an end, but a beginning!

Supposedly distinct, but actually quite similar, both *Alice* and *Sylvie and Bruno* offer a form of philosophical integration between otherwise purely theoretic and pragmatic worldviews, by means of a creative dialectic between the temporal and the eternal. As the reader is guided to the gestalt that all things are composed of an interplay between constants and variables, honest inquiry is invited, rendering the twin dangers of doctrinal fundamentalism and spiritual relativism equally impotent.

REFLECTIONS

The philosopher, as conceived by Plato is an ardent Lover. He lives all his earthly life in a trembling hope, and, out of his hope, sees visions, and prophesies.[273]

*T*he foregoing chapters were an attempt to explore the "curiosities" in the children's literature of Lewis Carroll. Looking at Carroll from an archetypal, as opposed to purely biographical, perspective, allowed me to offer another approach to deconstructing the Carroll Myth. In philosophically recontextualizing Carroll, the man behind the myths began to emerge. It became obvious that myth, in its most primary sense, was as essential to Carroll as it was to Plato. As I began to see the structure of the myth that Carroll was making, the myths that had surrounded him fell away quite naturally. Rather than merely being the subject of the myths, Carroll became a myth-maker. The myth he crafted, however, was neither social nor sexual... it was spiritual. Many of the myths that surrounded Carroll sprung up, in fact, out of a failure to understand Victorian esoteric trends. What has been referred to as the nineteenth century universality of a fad for child prodigies was not actually a fad at all. The Victorian Cult of the Child was, more accurately, a reappearance of the Orphic theogony for the belief in a divine child. In Orphism, the belief was illustrated by the existence of an actual cult that took the Child for the centre of its worship and caused its adorers to give to it as offerings the

273 J. A. Stewart, *The Myths of Plato* (Hertford, England: Stephan Austin and Sons Ltd., 1905), 303.

sort of gifts that may most naturally be supposed to please him/her, namely children's playthings.[274] In order for the divine child to mature into his or her full potential, initiation was required. As has been discussed, the concept of initiation was central to both ancient and nineteenth century mystery schools. The thrust of the initiatory process was for the candidate, through a series of trials, to obtain a direct experience of, as opposed to doctrinal instruction about, divinity. Alice, Carroll's symbol of the divine child, visited the underworld, as an initiatory candidate, as a part of the process of achieving *gnosis*. Such knowledge was not the result of sense-perception nor reason. It stood in contrast to them.[275] "Rather it was a special mental enlightenment, the gift of God, which freed men from the illusions of sense and gave them insight into reality and the purpose of existence."[276]

Carroll had been cultivated toward the priesthood from infancy and was expected, as a condition of his residency at Christ Church, to proceed to holy orders within four years of obtaining a master's degree. He, however, demonstrated reluctance to do this. After delaying the process for some time, he eventually took deacon's orders in 1861. When the time came, however, for Carroll to proceed to full orders, he appealed to the dean for permission not to proceed. This violated college rules and he was advised that it was probable that he would have to leave his job if he refused to take orders. Carroll never proceeded to full orders and Dean Liddell, for reasons unknown, permitted him to remain at the college. Although there is no conclusive evidence as to why Carroll declined the priesthood, it is quite likely that he was

274 W. K. C. Guthrie, *Orpheus and Greek Religion* (New York: W.W. Norton and Company, Inc., 1966).

275 *Corpus Hermetica,* x. 9.

276 Harold Willoughby, *Pagan Regeneration* (Chicago: The University of Chicago Press, 1929), 218.

entertaining serious doubts about the Anglican church. Further, as I have suggested in the foregoing chapters, it is most conceivable that his interest and involvement in the nineteenth century Platonic revival, as well as in the subsequent theosophical movement, substantially changed his spiritual direction. The exoteric structure, for him, of the Anglican church may well have been supplanted by esoteric insight. Rather than *knowing about* (*episteme*) truth, Carroll chose a path through which he could *know* (*gnosis*) Truth. This being so, Carroll chose to sing a new song. Instead of dogmatic liturgy, he sang the theosophist's intellectual hymn to Love and preached from carefully crafted allegory instead of from a pulpit.

One of the criticisms of applying this type of interpretation to Carroll's writings is the challenge that perhaps he did not intend for the stories to be esoteric allegories at all... but, rather, simply re-introductions of much older and more traditional literary motifs. Nonetheless, whether Carroll intentionally interjected philosophical content into his tales or not, it is there. Perhaps my discovery of it reflects my personal interaction with the material. Mathematicians feel that they uncover arithmetical theories when they dig into the *Alice* books, analysts identify what appear to them to be psychological theories, and historians are satisfied that there are socio-political satires woven into the tales. In each of these examples, the reader's particular area of interest and expertise informs his or her response to the text. I brought my interest in philosophy to Carroll's writings and it was a factor in how I responded to them. If we consider the text to be *Thou* and me to be *I*, the resulting *I–Thou* relationship would, naturally, have an element of subjectivity. With this as a caveat, I nonetheless feel that I have constructed a strong preliminary case for a Carroll whose mysticism coloured every aspect of his life. The mystical consciousness considers unity as both an internal and external focus as it seeks the truth about reality. The mystic goes beyond specific religious dogmas, espousing an inclusive and universal perspective that rises above doctrinal differences. Generally approached through a purification process, the mystic seeks to transcend his internal duality that constrains his direct experience of the divine.

The potential of a transcendent heroic self was traditionally psychologically detailed in powerful myths such as, for example, Theseus and Odysseus. In his own particular way, Carroll turns Alice into Odysseus journeying home to Ithaca. The hero's journey always involves the departure, an initiation and the return. The process of becoming conscious requires forming unity out of a pre-existent state of fragmentation. This is achieved through an integration of the ego with the more authentic self, forming a transcendent wholeness. This struggle to achieve a transcendent wholeness, the act of self-recollection, is the heroic struggle. Similar to the Platonic doctrine of *anamnesis,* the hero is required to gather together what is scattered, of all the things in him/her that have never been properly related, and to come to terms with him/herself with a view toward achieving full consciousness.[277] Alice, as an alter-ego for Carroll's transcendent heroic self, underwent a gentle initiation in Wonderland so that Carroll could share, discretely, his secret of *gnosis.* Heeding the advice, written centuries earlier by Roger Bacon,[278] Carroll concealed his secret carefully, leaving it so that it could be understood only by the efforts of the studious and wise.

---

277 Carl Jung, The Collected Works, vol. 11. Eds. Herbert Read, Michael Fordham and Gerhard Adler. Trans. R. F. C. Hull. (London: Bollingen Press, 1933), 263.

278 Roger Bacon, Wisdom of Keeping Secrets (c. 1260).

The Works of Charles Lutwidge Dodgson

MATHEMATICAL WORKS

1860   *A Syllabus of Plane Algebraic Geometry*
This book provides an outline and/or plan of study for a course in algebraic geometry, as well as some notes on Euclid. It is an impressive work, representing hours of research and analysis.

1861   *The Formula of Plane Geometry*
This book was published after an immense amount of work and contains a full collection of geometric formulas.

1866   *Condensation of Determinants*
This single volume work comprises a collection of symbols and a cycle of examples.

1867   *An Elementary Treatise on Determinants*
This work is a four-volume study of algebraic geometry. By Dodgson's own admission, it was a 'grand looking' accomplishment.

1868   *Formulae in Algebra for Responsions*
This text contains an array of notes, as well as a collection of formula, on algebra.

1874   *Euclid, Book V, Proved Algebraically*
As its name implies, Dodgson set about providing functional algebraic proof for the Fifth Book of Euclid so far as it relates to commensurate magnitudes, to which is prefixed a summary of all the necessary algebraic operations, arranged in order of difficulty.

1875   *Examples of Arithmetic*
This is a text of pure mathematics, with an outline of examples and proofs.

1879   *Euclid and His Modern Rivals*
Written in the form of a play, this script offers a defence of Euclid over the nineteenth century non-Euclidean geometries offered by Lobatchevsky, Riemann and Cayley.

1882   *Euclid, Books I and II*
In this text Dodgson again examines and supports the Euclidean approach to geometry. He wrote it specifically for circulation among the mathematical academic community.

1887   *The Game of Logic*
This humorous volume represents an attempt to explain formal logic by a board and counter method. It was intended for older scholars or adults, and the absurdity of the propositions make it entertaining reading.

1888   *Curiosa Mathematica, Part I: A New Theory of Parallels*
This book is a serious critical appraisal of the controversial Twelfth Axiom of Euclid.

1893   *Curiosa Mathematica, Part II (Pillow Problems)*
This book contains 72 problems, mostly in algebra, plane geometry, and/or trigonometry. All of the problems were invented and solved in the dark and not committed to paper until the next morning.

1893   *Syzygies and Lanrick: A Word-Puzzle and a Game for Two Players*

This text incorporated two word-games of Dodgson's own imagination, both of which had appeared separately as magazine articles in *The Lady* and the *Monthly Packet* respectively.

1896   *Symbolic Logic: Part I: Elementary*
This book is Dodgson's attempt to popularize formal logic, chiefly through the use of diagrams. He adopted a humorous style and was inventive in making the propositions intriguing, but did not extend the work by syllogisms.

THE OXFORD SQUIBS AND PAMPHLETS

1865   *American Telegrams*
A squib embodying contemporary Christ Church proceedings in the form of mock American news.

1865   *The New Method of Evaluation as Applied to Pi*
A squib on the controversy over the salary of Benjamin Jowett.

1865   *The Dynamics of a Parti-cle*
A squib about the Oxford elections of 13–18 July 1865.

1866   *The Elections to the Hebdomadal Council*
An assault on the developing materialism of the Oxford Liberals.

1867   *The Deserted Parks*
A parody of Goldsmith's *Deserted Village* which represented Dodgson's anonymous response to the decree that the University parks should be partly given over to the game of cricket.

1868   *The Offer of the Clarendon Trustees*: a satire where Dodgson set out the requirements of the Department of Mathematics for "re-roofed buildings" in which a variety of mathematical occupations such as a room for "reduced fractions to their lowest terms" and a cellar for "keeping lowest terms when found" could be carried out.

1872   *The New Belfry at Christ Church, Oxford: A Monograph by D.C.L.*
A pamphlet about the expense of reconstruction on the campus. Although this tract was published anonymously, its authorship was an open secret.

1873   *The Vision of the Three T's: A Threnody by the Author of 'The New Belfry'*
The three T's are tunnel, trench and tea-chest and the squib is a dramatic parody of *The Complete Angler*.

1874   *The Blank Cheque, A Fable*
The subject was the decision of convocation to build the new Examination Schools in the site of the Angel Inn and to leave the matter entirely in the hands of a nine-man executive committee without any broader input.

1874   *Objections, submitted to the Governing Body of Christ Church, Oxford, against certain proposed alterations in the Great Quadrangle*
This squib was partly responsible for the decision not to build cloisters in Tom Quad.

1874   *Suggestions as to the Best Method of Taking Votes*
A pamphlet about voter distribution methods.

1874   *Where More Than Two Issues are to be Voted on*
A pamphlet about voting methodically.

1875   *Some Popular Fallacies about Vivisection*
Originally published in *The Fortnightly Review*, was about the unnecessary infliction of pain for mere academic interest.

1876   *Professorship of Comparative Philology*
A pamphlet dealing with the salary of Max Müller.

1876   *Fame's Penny Trumpet*: in poem format, this pamphlet constitutes an attack on "little men of little souls" who valued money over learning. Vivisectors, too, receive a share of the general condemnation in this vitriolic verse.

1877   *Memoria Technica*: described a complicated method of learning as opposed to the rote method.

1878   *Word Links*: was an earlier version of the game *Doublets,* which Dodgson published the next year.

1884   *The Profits of Authorship*: a pamphlet which was intended to expose high bookseller markups and profits to the general public.

1884   *Lawn Tennis Tournaments*: a pamphlet which argued against the method of scoring tennis. His objections are now incorporated into the modern "seeding" systems employed at Wimbleton and elsewhere.

1884   *Parliamentary Elections* and *The Principles of Parliamentary Representation*: present a model of a logically rigorous political system in favour of proportional representation.

1884   *Twelve Months in a Curatorship*: a parody on a curatorship that Dodgson held in The Common Room at Oxford.

1886   *Three Years in a Curatorship:* a pamphlet about ventilation, light and furniture of The Common Room.

1889   *Curiosissima Curatoria:* a spoof in which Dodgson recorded some of the business of his nine years curatorship.

1890   *Circular Billiards*: describes rules for the playing of billiards on a round table with cushions but no pockets or spots.

1890   *Eight or Nine Wise Words About Letter-Writing:* a method for the systematic filing of correspondence.

I M A G I N A T I V E   L I T E R A T U R E
(A S   L E W I S   C A R R O L L)

1865   *Alice's Adventures in Wonderland*
This book became Carroll's most popular imaginative work. The tale adopts the apparent literary device of a dream convention which had been popular in the English literature of the Middle Ages when *Piers the*

Plowman fell asleep "Under a brode banke bi a bornes side" and the dreamers in *Pearl, Dream of the Rood,* and *Pilgrim's Progress* slept through visions of overwhelming religious significance.

1869   *Phantasmagoria and Other Poems*
The focal point of this volume is a previously unpublished, whimsical poem in seven cantos, about a friendly ghost who expounded "Hys Fyve Rules" for haunting, and points out that the things ghosts do are by no means enjoyable.

1871   *Through the Looking-Glass and What Alice Found There*
Carroll described this book as "the sequel volume of *Alice*", as it comprised a natural adjunct to his earlier *Alice's Adventures in Wonderland.*

1876   *The Hunting of the Snark*
This is a poem in three "fits": *The Landing, The Hunting* and *The Vanishing.* Despite Carroll's assertion that he did not know whether or not the poem contained any hidden significance, it is impossible to ignore certain references to the subjects of his Oxford squibs.

1883   *Rhyme? and Reason?*
This book was a new and more sophisticated version of the illustrated edition of *Phantasmagoria,* and contained the whole of *The Hunting of the Snark* with illustrations, *Fame's Penny Trumpet* and *Tema con Variazioni.*

1885   *A Tangled Tale*
This book consists of ten puzzles of "knots" which had previously been published by Charlotte M. Yonge in the *Monthly Packet,* with the answers, between April 1880 and March 1885.

1889   *Sylvie and Bruno*
Carroll said of *Sylvie and Bruno* that he entertained the hope of "suggesting some thoughts which would be in harmony with the graver cadences of life." Carroll bases the story on an intricately developed series of hypotheses that are religious and moral in content.

1893   *Sylvie and Bruno Concluded*

This volume is a sequel to the above.

1893　*A Logical Paradox* and *What the Tortoise said to Achilles,* in *Mind*

These articles were parodies aimed at promoting an innovative system of logic. As a logician, these tracts show Carroll to be years ahead of his time in sophistication of thought.

1898　*Three Sunsets and Other Poems*

Published posthumously, this represents an illustrated collection of poems from the author's "sunset years."

Questions Behind the Looking-Glass

A Carrollian Introduction to Philosophy

*A*ppendix B represents a creative, interdisciplinary approach for teaching Introductory Philosophy, using Lewis Carroll's *Alice* books as a launching point. Designed to provide an introduction to philosophy, a survey approach, with emphasis on epistemology and metaphysics, is employed. The course is geared to be appropriate for use with first-year college students and/or high school honors students. Selected modules from the accompanying syllabus were field tested on several types of student audiences. After each test, the learning objectives and methodology were revised to reflect the feedback received from the group participants. Through this interactive process, the course has evolved in ways that offer room for spontaneity, accommodates diverse learning styles, and provides a stimulating preliminary approach to some of the major problems of philosophy.

In the syllabus, references to primary philosophical works have been made in standard notation and any edition can, therefore, be used. The secondary, critical texts cited have been noted by specific edition. These editions, thus, must be conformed to in order for the page references to be accurate. For the Carrollian texts, I chose the 1998 Oxford University Press edition of *Alice in Wonderland* and *Through the Looking-Glass and What Alice Found There* because of its integrity toward Carroll's original syntax, its meticulous reproductions of the original Tenniel illustrations, its inclusion of essential annotations, and its economic availability. Of course, other editions of *Alice in Wonderland* and *Through the Looking-Glass* could be substituted, as appropriate, and the page references edited accordingly. I have also cross-referenced learning competencies in the syllabus with material from this book, for use with more sophisticated populations. It is not intended that the course facilitator will utilize all of the suggested materials, but will, instead, have a smorgasbord of choices to use, according to the sophistication level of his or her population.

It is my contention that this kind of approach provides a creative example of the benefits available through integrated, interdisciplinary methods of teaching within the humanities. The possibilities are, in fact, open-ended and the potential for introducing critical thinking skills into a wider range of course offerings is enhanced. The Carrollian influence liberates the new philosophy student to feel free to ask any question, and to consider any possibility, without the restrictive predictability of everyday life. I chose to capitalize upon this sense of free— even fantastical!—inquiry, in fact, by interjecting a few tenets of postmodern avant-garde ideology into the format. This highlights the contemporary significance of traditional philosophical questions and introduces new potential frontiers. In sum, it strikes me that this is a philosophy course that Lewis Carroll himself might very well have enjoyed!

Questions Behind the Looking-Glass:
A Carrollian Introduction to Philosophy

COURSE DESCRIPTION: An introduction to the perennial problems of philosophy, from the vantage point of the Cheshire-Cat, Humpty Dumpty and the Gryphon! The contributions of Plato, Aristotle, Plotinus, Descartes, Berkeley and Locke to the history of philosophical inquiry will be explored. Lewis Carroll's *Alice in Wonderland* and *Through the Looking-Glass and What Alice Found There* (Oxford University Press, 1998) provide the springboard for looking at intriguing epistemological and metaphysical questions. The nature of knowledge, as well as the nature and structure of reality will be challenged as students participate in Alice's adventures.

COURSE GOAL: To introduce the problems of philosophy, and important contributions to them, through analyses of selected passages from Lewis Carroll's *Alice* books, primary philosophical texts, secondary critical texts and contemporary investigations and inquiry.

COURSE OBJECTIVES: To make parallel readings between Carroll's satirical passages and selected sections from primary philosophical texts.

- To read and discuss secondary, critical texts pertinent to the philosophical positions.
- To become aware of the historical significance of philosophical inquiry.

• To become comfortable asking questions and engaging in critical thinking.

METHODOLOGY: Students will be asked to read from primary philosophical works, secondary critical works and Carroll's *Alice* books.

Reactions to the readings should be encouraged through mentored discussions, facilitated group interactions, written and dialogical exercises, and encouraged free association.

The syllabus is structured by topics and each topic is designed to require multiple readings and interactive sessions.

Students should be empowered to identify open-ended questions and issues through being encouraged to consider traditional philosophical concerns in light of selected avant-garde viewpoints.

MATERIALS:

I: Carrollian Literature:

Carroll, Lewis. *Alice's Adventures in Wonderland* and *Through the Looking-Glass: And What Alice Found There*. Edited with an Introduction and Notes by Roger Lancelyn Green. New York: Oxford University Press, 1998.

II: Primary Philosophical Texts:

Aristotle, *On Sense and the Sensible, On Dreams, On Memory and Reminiscence, Metaphysics*

Berkeley, *A Treatise concerning the Principles of Human Knowledge; Three Dialogues between Hylas and Philonous*

Descartes, *Meditations on First Philosophy; Principia Philosophiae* Locke, *An Essay Concerning Human Understanding* Plato, *Parmenides, Phaedo, Republic, Statesman, Theaetetus, Timaeus*, Plotinus, *The Enneads*

III: Secondary Critical Texts:

Audi, Robert. *Epistemology: A Contemporary Introduction to the Theory of Knowledge*. London and New York: Routledge, 1998.

Cottingham, John. *The Rationalists*. Oxford: Oxford University Press, 1988.

Gregory, John. *The Neoplatonists: A Reader*, 2nd ed. London and New York: Routledge, 1999.

Stumpf, Samuel Enoch and James Fieser. *Socrates to Sartre and Beyond: A History of Philosophy*, 7th edition. New York: McGraw-Hill, 2003.

Tarnas, Richard. *The Passion of the Western Mind*. New York: Ballantine Books, 1991.

Woolhouse, R.S. *The Empiricists*. Oxford: Oxford University Press, 1988.

IV: Contemporary/Alternative Investigations and Inquiry:

Austin, John H. *Zen and the Brain*. Cambridge, MA: The MIT Press, 1999.

Hagen, Steve. *How the World Can Be the Way It Is*. Wheaton, Ill.: Quest Books, 1998.

Ornstein, Robert. *The Evolution of Consciousness*. New York: Simon and Schuster, 1992.

Talbot, Michael. *The Holographic Universe*. New York: Harper Perennial, 1991.

Three Initiates. *The Kybalion: A Study of the Hermetic Philosophy of Ancient Egypt and Greece*. Chicago: The Yogi Publication Society, 1908.

V: Cross Referenced Material:

Ackerman, Sherry L. *Behind the Looking-Glass*. Newcastle upon Tyne, UK: Cambridge Scholars Publishing , 2008.

SYLLABUS

Topic #1: How do we know that what we perceive is real and that we are not merely dreaming?

Readings:

Carroll, *Looking-Glass*, pp. 167-168; 178-184; 242-244.

Carroll, *Alice*, pp. 103-111.

Aristotle, *On Dreams*. Descartes, *Meditation I*.

Plato, *Theaetetus*, 158-159.

Audi, *Epistemology*, pp. 14-30; 74-81.

Ornstein, *Evolution of Consciousness*, pp. 192-200.

Cross-references to *Behind the Looking-Glass*: pp. 20-22, 64, 97-98.

Interaction:

What constitutes knowledge?

What informs a claim to know?

Are claims to perception reliable?

Topic #2: What is the role of sensory experience in constituting knowledge?

Readings:

Carroll, *Alice*, pp. 12-18; 31-33; 75-78.

Aristotle, *On Sense and the Sensible*, chapters 1 and 6.

Berkeley, *Principles*, 1-8.

Descartes, *Meditation VI*: 1-7

Locke, *Human Understanding*, Book I: chapters I-III; Book II, chapter I.

Plato, *Theaetetus*, 184-196.

Audi, *Epistemology*, pp. 31-37; 45-49.

Stumpf and Fieser, *Socrates to Sartre*, pp.49-59; 82-90; 226-234; 252-257; 260-266.

Woolhouse, *The Empiricists*, pp. 74-106.

Hagen, *How the World Can Be the Way It Is*, pp. 58-65. Cross-reference to *Behind the Looking-Glass*: pp. 41-49, 69-71, 77-78, 97, 102-103.

Interaction:
  What is Rationalism?
  What is Empiricism?
  What were the historical imperatives for the development
    of these theories of knowledge?
  What significance do these theories have for today?

Topic #3: What is memory?
Readings:
  Carroll, *Looking-Glass*, pp. 132-133; 174-176.
  Aristotle, *On Memory and Reminiscence* Plotinus, *Fourth
    Ennead*, Tractate 6
  Audi, *Epistemology*, pp. 53-70.
  Austin, *Zen and the Brain*, pp, 259-262.
  Ornstein, *Evolution of Consciousness*, pp. 181-191.
  Talbot, *Holographic Universe*, pp. 11-31.
Cross-reference to *Behind the Looking-Glass*: pp. 59, 92.
Interaction:
  What, essentially, is the relationship between events in the
    brain and those private, subjective, introspective
    experiences that together constitute our inner mental
    life?
  Discuss epiphenomenalism. What are its counter-
    positions?

Topic #4: What is the nature of time?
Readings:
  Carroll, *Alice*, pp. 62-64.
  Carroll, *Looking-Glass*, pp. 144-145; 173-178.
  Aristotle, *Physics,* Book IV, Section C.
  Locke, *Human Understanding*, Chapter XIV.
  Plato, *Timaeus*, 37 c-e.
  Plotinus, *Third Ennead*, Tractate 7.
  Stumpf and Fieser, *Socrates to Sartre*, 71-74.

Gregory, *The Neoplatonists*, pp. 59-61; 88.

Talbot, *Holographic Universe*, pp. 197-208.

Cross-reference to *Behind the Looking-Glass*: pp.53-62.

Interaction:

How is time related to mind?

What are the differences between relational and absolute theories of time?

Topic #5: Where does the day begin? Exploring the Absolute and the Relative.

Readings:

Carroll, *Looking-Glass*, pp. 141-143; 169-172.

Berkeley, *Dialogues,* First Dialogue.

Plato, *Republic*, Book 6, 509d-513e; Book 7, 514a-517c.

Plotinus, *Sixth Ennead*, Tractate 9, Sections 1-6.

Tarnas, *Western Mind*, pp. 6-12; 41-47.

Audi, *Epistemology,* pp. 259-264.

Three Initiates, *Kybalion*, Chapter X.

Cross-reference to *Behind the Looking-Glass*: pp. 53- 56, 122-131.

Interaction:

In value theory, the absolute takes center stage in discussions between 'absolute values' and 'relative values.' Is there something upon which we can base our actions that does not change no matter what the circumstances? Are the laws of nature absolute? Are the laws of God absolute?

Topic #6: Is gravity absolute?

Readings:

Carroll, *Alice*, pp. 9-12.

Carroll, *Looking-Glass*, pp. 212-213.

Aristotle, *Physics*, Book II, Section A.

Descartes, *Principia Philosophiae*, Part IV

Tarnas, *Western Mind*, pp. 267-271.

Hagen, *How the World Can Be the Way It Is*, Chapter 8.

Cross-references to *Behind the Looking-Glass*: pp. 62-64.

Interaction:

Do you think that Einstein's general theory of relativity seems to have a loophole that would allow for the possibility of negative gravity from an object with a negative mass?

Topic #7: What are some other theories that have shaped Western thinking?

Realist Theories of Universals:

Readings:

Carroll, *Looking-Glass*, pp. 127-129.

Aristotle, *Metaphysics* 1028b-1029b 10.

Plato, *Republic*, 517b-c4.

Stumpf, *Socrates to Sartre*, pp. 150-151.

Cross-reference with *Behind the Looking-Glass*, pp. 15.

Nominalism:

Readings:

Carroll, *Looking-Glass*, 152-158; 185-197.

Berkeley, *Principles*, Introduction.

Descartes, *Principles*, Part I, Article 57.

Locke, *Human Understanding*, Book III, Chapter III.

Stumpf, *Socrates to Sartre*, pp. 151-152.

Cross-reference with *Behind the Looking-Glass*, pp. 49-50, 72-74.

Resemblance:

Readings:

Carroll, *Alice*, pp. 46-49. Carroll, *Looking-Glass*, p. 185.

Plato, *Republic*, 514-517, 596a-e; *Phaedo*, 74-76, 100c-d; *Parmenides*, 131a-135e.

Cross-reference with *Behind the Looking-Glass*, pp. 50, 72-74, 129.

Coherence vs. Correspondence:
Readings:
    Carroll, *Looking-Glass*, pp. 204-205; 226-227.
    Aristotle, *Metaphysics*, 1011b 10-25.
    Audi, *Epistemology,* pp. 238-242.
    Stumpf, *Socrates to Sartre,* pp. 398-400.
Cross-reference with *Behind the Looking-Glass*, pp. 6.

Topic #8: Where does all of this leave *me?* Who *am* I? Do I *exist?*
Readings:
    Carroll, *Alice*, pp. 18-20; 31-33; 40-46; 92-94.
    Carroll, *Looking-Glass*, pp. 155-158.
    Descartes, *Meditation II.*
    Plotinus, *Fourth Ennead*, Tractate 9.
    Audi, *Epistemology*, 282-294.
    Gregory, *The Neoplatonists*, pp. 81-82.
    Stumpf, *Socrates to Sartre*, pp. 487-490.
    Hagens, *How the World Can Be the Way It Is*, pp. 284-295.
    Talbot, *Holographic Universe*, pp. 32-55.
Cross-reference with *Behind the Looking-Glass*, pp. 67-68, 92-93, 103- 104.
Interaction:
    How can I know that "I am"?

Bibliography

Ackerman, Robert. *Theories of Knowledge: An Introduction*. New York: McGraw Hill, 1965.

Agrippa, Henricus Cornelius. *Henry Cornelius Agrippa his Fourth Book of Occult Philosophy: Arbetel of Magick*. Translated by Robert Turner. London, 1655.

Alighieri, Dante. *Inferno*. Translated by Anthony Esolen. New York: Modern Library, 2002.

Amor, Anne Clark. *Lewis Carroll: A Biography*. London: Dent Publishing, 1979.

Bacon, Roger. *The Letter of Roger Bacon Concerning the Marvelous Power of Art And of Nature and Concerning the Nullity of Magic*. Translated by Tenney L. Davis. London, c. 1252.

Ball, W. W. Rouse. *Mathematical Recreations and Essays*. London: MacMillan and Co., Ltd., 1892.

Benn, Alfred William. *The History of English Rationalism in the Nineteenth Century,* vol. 1. London: Longmans, Green, and Co., 1906.

Berkeley, George. *The Works of George Berkeley,* vols. 1 and 2. London: Thomas Tegg, 1843.

——. *Principles of Human Knowledge and Three Dialogues*. Edited by Howard Robinson. New York: Oxford University Press, 1999.

Besant, Annie. *The Ideals of Theosophy*. Adyar Madras, India: The Theosophist's Office, 1912.

Bigg, C. *Chief Ancient Philosophies: Neoplatonism.* London: Society for Promoting Christian Knowledge, 1895.

Blavatsky, Helena Petrovna. *The Secret Doctrine.* London: The Theosophical Society, 1888.

Bloom, Harold, ed. *Modern Critical Views: Lewis Carroll.* New York: Chelsea House Publishers, 1987.

Burkett, Walter. *Lore and Science in Ancient Pythagoreanism.* Translated by Edwin L. Minar, Jr. Cambridge, MA: Harvard University Press, 1972.

Capra, Fritjof. *The Tao of Physics.* Boston: Shambhala Publications, Inc., 1975.

Carroll, Lewis. *Alice's Adventures in Wonderland* and *Through the Looking-Glass: And What Alice Found There.* Edited with an Introduction and Notes by Roger Lancelyn Green. New York: Oxford University Press, 1998.

——. *Sylvie and Bruno* and *Sylvie and Bruno Concluded:* 2 vols. London: MacMillan and Co., 1889.

——. *The Hunting of the Snark.* Introduction by Martin Gardner. London: Penguin Classics, 1998.

Case, Paul Foster. *The True and Invisible Rosicrucian Order.* York Beach, Maine: Samuel Weiser, Inc., 1985.

Cassirer, Ernst. *The Platonic Renaissance in England.* Translated by James P. Pettegrove. Austin: University of Texas Press, 1953.

Chaney, Earlyne. *Lost Secrets of the Mystery Schools.* Upland, CA: Astara, 1992.

Clifford, William K. *William K. Clifford, Mathematical Papers.* Edited by Robert Tucker. Introduction by H.J.S. Smith. New York: Chelsea, 1968.

Cohen, Morton N. and Roger Lancelyn Green, eds. *The Letters of Lewis Carroll:* vols. 1 and 2. New York: Oxford University Press, 1979.

Cole, John R. *The Olympian Dream and Youthful Rebellion of René Descartes.* Urbana and Chicago: University of Illinois Press, 1992.

Collingwood, Stuart Dodgson. *Life and Letters of Lewis Carroll.* New York: The Century Co., 1898.

Copenhaver, Brian, ed. *Hermetica: The Greek Corpus Hermeticum and the Latin Asclepius*. Boston: Cambridge University Press, 1992.

Copleston, Frederick. *The History of Philosophy*, vol. 5. Edited by Edmund F. Sutcliffe. Westminster, Maryland: The Newman Press, 1959.

Cottingham, John. *The Rationalists*. Oxford, New York: Oxford University Press, 1988.

Couliano, Ioan P. *The Tree of Gnosis: Gnostic Mythology from Early Christianity to Modern Nihilism*. San Francisco: Harper Collins, 1992.

Cudworth, Ralph. *A Treatise Concerning Eternal and Immutable Morality*. Edited by Sarah Hutton. Cambridge: Cambridge University Press, 2005.

———. *True Intellectual System of the Universe*. Glacier National Park, Montana: Kessinger Publishing, 2004.

Davis, Andrew Jackson. *The Principles of Nature, Her Divine Revelations*. New York: S.S. Lyon and Wm. Fishbough, 1850.

de Purucker, G. *Fundamentals of Esoteric Philosophy*. Pasadena, California: Theosophical University Press, 1932.

Descartes, René. *The Philosophical Writings of Descartes*, vol. 1. Edited by John Cottingham, Robert Stoothoff and Dugald Murdoch. Cambridge: Cambridge University Press, 1985.

———. *The Philosophical Writings of Descartes*, vol. 2. . Edited by John Cottingham, Robert Stoothoff and Dugald Murdoch. Cambridge: Cambridge University Press, 1985.

Docherty, John. "The Literary Products of the Lewis Carroll-MacDonald Friendship". Reviewed by Charlie Lovett. *Knight Letter 48*. Autumn, 1994.

Dodgson, Charles L. *Curiosa Mathematica, Part I: A New Theory of Parallels*. London: Macmillan and Co., 1888.

———. *Euclid, Book V, Proved Algebraically*. London: James Parker and Co., 1874.

———. *Euclid and His Modern Rivals*. London: Macmillan and Co., 1885.

———. *Euclid and His Modern Rivals*. Introduction by H. S. M. Coxeter. New York: Dover Publications, Inc., 1973.

——. *Examples of Arithmetic*. Oxford: E. P. Hall and J. H. Stacy, 1874.

Eddington, Arthur Stanley. *Space, Time and Gravitation, An Outline of the General Relativity Theory*. Cambridge: Cambridge University Press, 1920.

Empson, William. "The Child as Swain". *Alice in Wonderland*, 2nd ed. Edited by Donald J. Gray. New York: W.W. Norton & Company, 1992.

Farwell, Ruth and Christopher Knee. "The End of the Absolute: A Nineteenth Century Contribution to General Relativity." *Studies in the History and Philosophy of Science*. March 1990, 21.

Fideler, David. *Jesus Christ, Sun of God: Ancient Cosmology and Early Christian Symbolism*. Wheaton, Illinois: Quest Books, 1993.

Gardner, Martin, ed. *The Annotated Alice*. New York: Clarkson N. Potter, Inc., 1960.

——. *The Annotated Snark*. New York: Simon and Schuster, 1962.

Gauld, Alan. *The Founders of Psychical Research*. London: Routledge & K. Paul, 1968.

Godwin, Joscelyn. *Arktos: The Polar Myth*. Grand Rapids, Michigan: Phanes Press, 1993.

——. *The Theosophical Enlightenment*. Albany: State University of New York Press, 1994.

Gray, Donald J. ed. *Authoritative Texts of Alice in Wonderland/ Through the Looking-Glass/Hunting of the Snark: Backgrounds and Essays in Criticism*. New York: W. W. Norton and Co., 1992.

Greenacre, Phyllis. *Swift and Carroll: A Psychoanalytic Study of Two Lives*. New York: International University Press, 1955.

Gregory, John. *The Neoplatonists*. London: Kyle Cathie Ltd., 1991.

Grosbras, Pascale Renaud. *"La method structurale dans Sylvie et Bruno"(The Structural Method in Sylvie and Bruno)*, *Lewis Carroll, jeux et enjeux critique*. Edited by Michel Morel. Presses Universitaires de Nancy, 2003.

Guiliano, Edward, ed. *Lewis Carroll Observed: A Collection of Unpublished Photographs, Drawings, Poetry and New Essays*. New York: Clarkson N. Potter, Inc., 1976.

——. *Soaring with the Dodo: Essays on Lewis Carroll's Life and Art.* Charlottesville, VA: University Press of Virginia, 1982.

Guthrie, Kenneth Sylvan. *The Pythagorean Sourcebook and Library.* Grand Rapids, Michigan: Phanes Press, 1987.

Guthrie, W. K. C. *Orpheus and Greek Religion.* New York: W.W. Norton and Company, Inc., 1966.

Hall, Manly P. *Lectures on Ancient Philosophy: An Introduction to the Study and Application of Rational Procedure.* Los Angeles: The Hall Publishing Co., 1929.

Harper, George Mills. *The Neoplatonism of William Blake.* Chapel Hill: University of North Carolina Press, 1961.

Harrison, C. G. *The Transcendental Universe.* Introduction by Christopher Bamford. Hudson, New York: Lindisfarne Press, 1993.

Heath, Peter. *The Philosopher's Alice.* New York: St. Martin's Press, 1974.

Hermes Trismegistus [pseud.]. *Mercurii Trismegisti Pymander, de potestate et sapientia Dei.* Translated by Marsilio Ficino. Edited by Jacques Lefèvre d'Ètaples and Michael Isengrin. Basel, Switzerland: 1532.

Hodson, Geoffry and Alexander Horne. *Some Experiments in Four Dimensional Vision.* London: Rider and Co., 1933.

Hutchins, Robert Maynard , ed. *Great Books of the Western World,* vol. 31. Chicago: University of Chicago Press, 1952.

Huxley, Aldous. *The Perennial Philosophy.* New York and London: Harper & Brothers Publishers, 1945.

Jonas, Hans. *The Gnostic Religion.* Boston: Beacon Press, 1958.

Jung, Carl. *The Collected Works*, vol. 11. Edited by Herbert Read, Michael Fordham and Gerhard Adler. Translated by R. F. C. Hull. London: Bollingen Press, 1933.

Kennington, Richard. "Descartes' 'Olympia'". *Social Research* 28, no. 2. Summer, 1961.

Kingsley, William. *The Gnosis or Ancient Wisdom in the Christian Scriptures.* London: George Allen and Unwin Ltd., 1937.

Leach, Karoline. *In the Shadow of the Dreamchild: A New Understanding of Lewis Carroll.* London: Peter Owens Publishing, 1999.

Mallet, Charles Edward. *A History of the University of Oxford (18th and 19th Centuries),* vol. 3. London: Methuen Co., Ltd, 1927.

Mason, R. Osgood. *Telepathy and the Subliminal Self.* New York: Henry Holt and Co., 1899.

Newman, J. H. *Tract XC: On Certain Passages in the XXXIX Articles.* London: Rivingtons, 1865.

Oderberg, I. M. "The Sacred Pilgrim in Greek Thought". *Sunrise Magazine.* November, 1977.

Paley, William. *Evidences of the Existence and Attributes of the Deity, Collected from the Appearances of Nature.* London: F. C. and J. Rivington, 1819.

Phillips, Robert, ed. *Aspects of Alice.* New York: The Vanguard Press, Inc., 1971.

Plato. *The Works of Plato.* Translated by Floyer Sydenham and Thomas Taylor. London: R. Wilks, 1804.

——. *Plato: The Collected Dialogues.* Edited by Edith Hamilton and Huntington Cairns. Princeton: Princeton University Press, 1961.

Plotinus. *The Enneads.* Translated by Stephen Mackenna. New York: Larson Publications, 1992.

Poliakov, Leon. *The Aryan Myth: A History of Racist and Nationalist Ideas in Europe.* Translated by E. Howard. New York: Basic Books, 1971.

Proclus. *A Commentary on the First Book of Euclid's Elements.* Translated by Glenn R. Morrow. Princeton: Princeton University Press, 1992.

Raine, Kathleen and George Mills Harper, *Thomas Taylor The Platonist: Selected Writings.* Princeton: Princeton University Press, 1969.

Rackin, Donald. "Blessed Rage: Lewis Carroll and the Modern Quest for Order". *Alice in Wonderland,* 2nd ed. Edited by Donald Gray. New York: W. W. Norton & Company, 1992.

Ratsche, Christian. *The Encyclopedia of Psychoactive Plants.* Rochester, Vermont: Park Street Press, 2005.

Richards, Joan. *Mathematical Visions: The Pursuit of Geometry in Victorian England.* Boston: Harcourt Brace Jovanovitch, 1988.

Ripinsky-Naxon, Michael. *The Nature of Shamanism.* Albany: State University of New York Press, 1993.

Ritchie, A. D. *George Berkeley: A Reappraisal.* New York: Barnes and Noble, Inc., 1967.

Schrodter, Willy. *Geheimkunste der Rosenkreuzer* (1954). Translated to English as *A Rosicrucian Notebook.* York Beach, Maine: Samuel Weiser, 1992.

Sorensen, Roy. *A Brief History of the Paradox.* Oxford: Oxford University Press, 2003.

Stewart, John Alexander and others, eds. "Platonism in English Poetry". *English Literature and the Classics.* Oxford: Clarendon Press, 1912.

Stewart, John Alexander. *The Myths of Plato.* Hertford, England: Stephen Austin and Sons Ltd., 1905. Talbot, Michael. *The Holographic Universe.* New York: Harper Perennial, 1992.

Tarnas, Richard. *The Passion of the Western Mind.* New York: Ballantine Books, 1991.

Taylor, Alexander L. *The White Knight: A Study of C. L. Dodgson (Lewis Carroll).* Philadelphia: Dufour Editions, 1963.

Taylor, Thomas. *A Dissertation on the Eleusinian and Bacchic Mysteries.* New York: J. W. Bouton, 1875.

Theosophy, Vol. 27, No. 4, February, 1939.

Three Initiates. *The Kybalion: A Study of the Hermetic Philosophy of Ancient Egypt and Greece.* Chicago: The Yogi Publication Society, 1908.

Underhill, Evelyn . *Mysticism.* New York: E. P. Dutton & Co., Inc., 1911.

——. *Practical Mysticism.* New York: E. P. Dutton & Co., Inc., 1915.

Waite, Arthur Edward. *The Real History of the Rosicrucians.* London: William Rider and Son, 1887.

Warren, William F. *Paradise Found: The Cradle of the Human Race at the North Pole.* Boston, MA: Houghton Mifflin & Co., 1885.

Wasson, R. Gordon , Stella Kramrisch, Jonathon Ott , and Carl A. P. Ruck. *Persephone's Quest: Entheogens and the Origins of Religion.* New Haven and London: Yale University Press, 1986.

Watts, Alan. "The Elemental Kingdoms", recorded at Big Sur: Esalen Institute Workshop, 1968.

Webb, James. *The Occult Underground.* Peru, Illinois: Open Court Publishing Co., 1974.

Wilberforce, Basil. *Mystic Immanence.* London: Elliot Stock, 1925.

Willoughby, Harold. *Pagan Regeneration.* Chicago: The University of Chicago Press, 1929.

Woolhouse, R. S. *The Empiricists.* Oxford: Oxford University Press, 1988.

Zukav, Gary. *The Dancing Wu Li Masters.* New York: Harper Collins Publishers, Inc., 1979.

Index

Alice's Adventures in Wonderland, by Lewis Carroll 2008

Through the Looking-Glass and What Alice Found There
by Lewis Carroll 2009

A New Alice in the Old Wonderland
by Anna Matlack Richards, 2009

New Adventures of Alice, by John Rae, 2010

Alice Through the Needle's Eye, by Gilbert Adair, 2012

Wonderland Revisited and the Games Alice Played There
by Keith Sheppard, 2009

Alice's Adventures under Ground, by Lewis Carroll 2009

The Nursery "Alice", by Lewis Carroll 2010

The Hunting of the Snark, by Lewis Carroll 2010

The Haunting of the Snarkasbord, by Alison Tannenbaum,
Byron W. Sewell, Charlie Lovett, and August A. Imholtz, Jr, 2012

Snarkmaster, by Byron W. Sewell, 2012

Alice's Adventures in Wonderland,
Retold in words of one Syllable by Mrs J. C. Gorham, 2010

Alice's Adventures in Wonderland,
Printed in the Nyctographic Square Alphabet, 2011

Behind the Looking-Glass: Reflections on the Myth of
Lewis Carroll, by Sherry L. Ackermann, 2012

Clara in Blunderland, by Caroline Lewis, 2010

Lost in Blunderland: The further adventures of Clara
by Caroline Lewis, 2010

John Bull's Adventures in the Fiscal Wonderland
by Charles Geake, 2010

The Westminster Alice, by H. H. Munro (Saki), 2010

Alice in Blunderland: An Iridescent Dream
by John Kendrick Bangs, 2010

Rollo in Emblemland, by J. K. Bangs & C. R. Macauley, 2010

Gladys in Grammarland, by Audrey Mayhew Allen, 2010

Alice's Adventures in Pictureland,
by Florence Adèle Evans, 2011

Eileen's Adventures in Wordland, by Zillah K. Macdonald, 2010

Phyllis in Piskie-land, by J. Henry Harris, 2012

The Admiral's Caravan, by Charles Edward Carryl, 2010

Davy and the Goblin, by Charles Edward Carryl, 2010

Alix's Adventures in Wonderland:
Lewis Carroll's Nightmare, by Byron W. Sewell, 2011

Álobk's Adventures in Goatland, by Byron W. Sewell, 2011

The Carrollian Tales of Inspector Spectre
by Byron W. Sewell, 2011

Alice's Adventures in An Appalachian Wonderland
Alice in Appalachian English, 2012

Crystal's Adventures in A Cockney Wonderland
Alice in Cockney Rhyming Slang, 2013

Alys in Pow an Anethow, *Alice* in Cornish, 2009

Alices Hændelser i Vidunderlandet, *Alice* in Danish, 2012

La Aventuroj de Alicio en Mirlando,
Alice in Esperanto, by E. L. Kearney, 2009

La Aventuroj de Alico en Mirlando,
Alice in Esperanto, by Donald Broadribb, 2012

Trans la Spegulo kaj kion Alico trovis tie,
Looking-Glass in Esperanto, by Donald Broadribb, 2012

Les Aventures d'Alice au pays des merveilles
Alice in French, 2010

Alice's Abenteuer im Wunderland, *Alice* in German, 2010

Nā Hana Kupanaha a ʻĀleka ma ka ʻĀina Kamahaʻo,
Alice in Hawaiian, 2012

Ma Loko o ke Aniani Kū a me ka Mea i Loaʻa iā ʻĀleka ma
Laila, *Alice* in Hawaiian, 2012

Eachtraí Eilíse i dTír na nIontas, *Alice* in Irish, 2007

Lastall den Scáthán agus a bhFuair Eilís Ann Roimpi
Looking-Glass in Irish, 2009

Le Avventure di Alice nel Paese delle Meraviglie
Alice in Italian, 2010

L's Aventuthes d'Alice en Êmèrvil'lie, *Alice* in Jèrriais, 2012

L'Travèrs du Mitheux et chein qu'Alice y dêmuchit,
Looking-Glass in Jèrriais, 2012

Alicia in Terra Mirabili, *Alice* in Latin, 2011

La aventuras de Alisia en la pais de mervelias
Alice in Lingua Franca Nova, 2012

Alice ehr Eventüürn in't Wunnerland
Alice in Low German, 2010

Contoyrtyssyn Ealish ayns Çheer ny Yindyssyn
Alice in Manx, 2010

Dee Erläwnisse von Alice em Wundalaund
Alice in Mennonite Low German, 2012

Ailice's Anters in Ferlielann, *Alice* in North-East Scots, 2012

L'Aventuros de Alis in Marvoland, *Alice* in Neo, 2012

Lès-Aventûres d'Alice ô Pèyis dès Mèrvèy,
Alice in Borain Picard, 2012

Ailice's Aventurs in Wunnerland, *Alice* in Scots, 2011

Eachdraidh Ealasaid ann an Tìr nan Iongantas,
Alice in Scottish Gaelic, 2012

Alice's Adventirs in Wonderlaand, *Alice* in Shetland Scots, 2012

Alices Äventyr i Sagolandet, *Alice* in Swedish, 2010

Alice's Carrànts in Wunnerlan, *Alice* in Ulster Scots, 2011

Ventürs jiela Lälid in Stunalän, *Alice* in Volapük, 2013

Lès-avirètes da Alice ô payis dès mèrvèyes,
Alice in Walloon, 2012

Anturiaethau Alys yng Ngwlad Hud, *Alice* in Welsh, 2010